THE 10 BEST
MENTAL TOUGHNESS EXERCISES

SAMMY FRANCO

Also by Sammy Franco

Cane Fighting
Double End Bag Training
The Heavy Bag Bible
The Widow Maker Compendium
Invincible: Mental Toughness Techniques for Peak Performance
Unleash Hell: A Step-by-Step Guide to Devastating Widow Maker Combinations
Feral Fighting: Advanced Widow Maker Fighting Techniques
The Widow Maker Program: Extreme Self-Defense for Deadly Force Situations
Savage Street Fighting: Tactical Savagery as a Last Resort
Heavy Bag Workout
Heavy Bag Combinations
Heavy Bag Training
The Complete Body Opponent Bag Book
Stand and Deliver: A Street Warrior's Guide to Tactical Combat Stances
Maximum Damage: Hidden Secrets Behind Brutal Fighting Combinations
First Strike: End a Fight in Ten Seconds or Less!
The Bigger They Are, The Harder They Fall
Self-Defense Tips and Tricks
Kubotan Power: Quick & Simple Steps to Mastering the Kubotan Keychain
Gun Safety: For Home Defense and Concealed Carry
Out of the Cage: A Guide to Beating a Mixed Martial Artist on the Street
Warrior Wisdom: Inspiring Ideas from the World's Greatest Warriors
War Machine: How to Transform Yourself Into a Vicious and Deadly Street Fighter
1001 Street Fighting Secrets
When Seconds Count: Self-Defense for the Real World
Killer Instinct: Unarmed Combat for Street Survival
Street Lethal: Unarmed Urban Combat

The 10 Best Mental Toughness Exercises (10 Best Series #5)
Copyright © 2017 by Sammy Franco
ISBN: 978-1-941845-49-3
Printed in the United States of America

Published by Contemporary Fighting Arts, LLC.
Visit us Online at: **SammyFranco.com**

Contents

"We are what we repeatedly do. Excellence, therefore, is not an act but a habit."

-Aristotle

Warning!

The author, publisher, and distributors of this book disclaim any liability from loss, injury, or damage, personal or otherwise, resulting from the information and procedures in this book. This book is for academic study only.

The information contained in this book is not designed to diagnose, treat, or manage any psychological or physical health conditions.

Before you begin any exercise or activity, both physical and mental, including those suggested in this book, it is important to check with your physician to see if you have any condition that might be aggravated by strenuous training.

How This Book Can Change Your Life

The 10 Best Mental Toughness Exercises contains battle-tested techniques and strategies for improving mental toughness in all aspects of life. It teaches you how to unlock the true power of your mind and achieve success in business, sports, high-risk professions, self-defense, fitness, and other peak performance activities.

However, you don't have to be an athlete or warrior to benefit from this unique mental toughness book. In fact, the mental skills featured in this indispensable program can be used by anyone who wants to reach their full potential in life.

Unlike other mental toughness books, The 10 Best Mental Toughness Exercises doesn't bog you down with dry theories, mind-numbing case studies, confusing jargon or pointless anecdotal stories. Instead, it's written in simple, easily understood language, so you can quickly learn and apply the mental skills and achieve personal success.

The 10 Best Mental Toughness Exercises has grit! It contains fresh and innovative training methods for developing and sharpening the essential building blocks of mental toughness. The techniques and exercises featured in this book are based on my 30+ years of research, training and teaching the martial arts and combat sciences. They have helped thousands of my students excel and achieve their personal goals, and I'm confident they will help you reach new levels of success.

In this book, you'll find step-by-step strategies for dealing with the debilitating fear and anxiety often associated with high-performance situations. In essence, it provides you with the mental body armor necessary to cope, perform and prevail from all forms of extreme adversity. By studying and practicing the concepts and principles in this book, you will feel a renewed sense of empowerment, enabling you to live life with greater self-confidence and personal freedom.

Finally, this book is just a small sampling of my unique mental toughness training program. If you would like to learn more, I strongly encourage you to read my other books, **The 10 Best Ways to Develop Your Killer Instinct** and **Invincible: Mental Toughness Techniques for the Street, Battlefield and Playing Field.**

Train hard!
Sammy Franco

Introduction
Contemporary Fighting Arts

The 10 Best Mental Toughness Exercises

Exploring Contemporary Fighting Arts

Before diving head first into this book, I'd like to first introduce you to my unique system of fighting, Contemporary Fighting Arts (CFA). I hope it will give you a greater understanding and appreciation of the material covered in this book. And for those of you who are already familiar with CFA, you can skip to the next chapter.

Contemporary Fighting Arts® (CFA), is a state-of-the-art combat system that was introduced to the world in 1983. This sophisticated and practical system of self-defense is designed specifically to provide efficient and effective methods to avoid, defuse, confront, and neutralize both armed and unarmed assailants in a variety of deadly situations and circumstances.

Unlike karate, kung-fu, mixed martial arts and the like, CFA is the first offensive-based American martial art that is specifically designed for the violence that plagues our cruel city streets. CFA dispenses with the extraneous and the impractical and focuses on real-life street fighting.

Every tool, technique and tactic found within the CFA system must meet three essential criteria for fighting: efficiency, effectiveness, and safety. Efficiency means that the techniques permit you to reach your combative objective quickly and economically. Effectiveness means that the elements of the system will produce the desired effect. Finally, Safety means that the combative elements provide the least amount of danger and risk for you - the fighter.

CFA is not about mind-numbing tournaments or senseless competition. It does not require you to waste time and energy practicing forms (katas) or other impractical rituals. There are no theatrical kicks or exotic techniques. Finally, CFA does not adhere blindly to tradition for tradition's sake. Simply put, it is a scientific yet pragmatic approach to staying alive on the streets.

CFA has been taught to people of all walks of life. Some include the U.S. Border Patrol, police officers, deputy sheriffs, security guards, military personnel, private investigators, surgeons, lawyers, college professors, airline pilots, as well as black belts, boxers, and kick boxers. CFA's broad appeal results from its ability to teach people how to really fight.

It's All In The Name!

Before discussing the three components that make up Contemporary Fighting Arts, it is important to understand how CFA acquired its unique name. To begin, the first word, "Contemporary," was selected because it refers to the system's modern, up-to-date orientation. Unlike traditional martial arts, CFA is specifically designed to meet the challenges of our modern world.

The second term, "Fighting," was chosen because it accurately describes the system's combat orientation. After all, why not just call it Contemporary Martial Arts? There are two reasons for this. First, the word "martial" conjures up images of traditional and impractical martial art forms that are antithetical to the system. Second, why dilute a perfectly functional name when the word "fighting" defines the system so succinctly? Contemporary Fighting Arts is about teaching people how to really fight.

Let's look at the last word, "Arts." In the subjective sense, "art" refers to the combat skills that are acquired through arduous study, practice, and observation. The bottom line is that effective street fighting skills will require consistent practice and attention. Take, for example, something as seemingly basic as an elbow strike, which will actually require hundreds of hours of practice to perfect.

The pluralization of the word "Art" reflects CFA's protean instruction. The various components of CFA's training (i.e., firearms training, stick fighting, ground fighting, natural body weapon mastery, and so on) have all truly earned their status as individual art forms and, as such, require years of consistent study and practice to perfect. To acquire a greater understanding of CFA, here is an overview of the system's three vital components: the physical, the mental, and the spiritual.

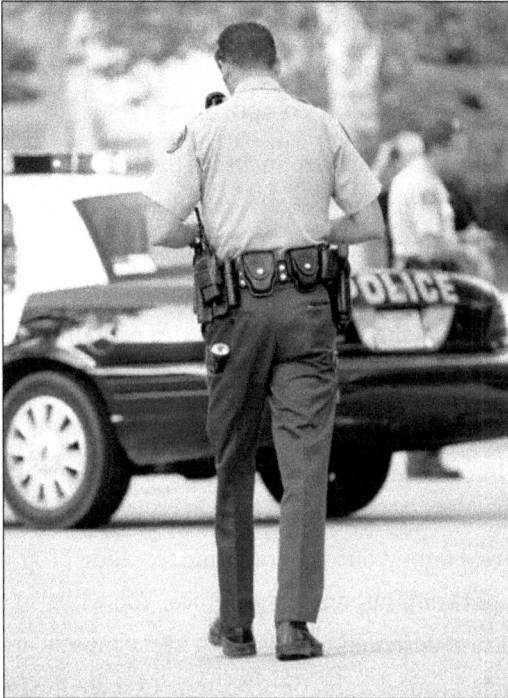

Police officers need practical and effective defensive tactics for dealing with violent street criminals. This is why many law enforcement officers seek out Contemporary Fighting Arts training.

The Physical Component

The physical component of CFA focuses on the physical development of a fighter, including physical fitness, weapon and technique mastery, and self-defense attributes.

Physical Fitness

If you are going to prevail in a street fight, you must be physically fit. It's that simple. In fact, you will never master the tools and skills of combat unless you're in excellent physical shape. On the average, you will have to spend more than an hour a day to achieve maximum fitness.

In CFA physical fitness comprises the following three broad components: cardiorespiratory conditioning, muscular/skeletal conditioning, and proper body composition.

The cardiorespiratory system includes the heart, lungs, and circulatory system, which undergo tremendous stress during the course of a street fight. So you're going to have to run, jog, bike, swim, or skip rope to develop sound cardiorespiratory conditioning. Each aerobic workout should last a minimum of 30 minutes and be performed at least four times per week.

The second component of physical fitness is muscular/skeletal conditioning. In the streets, the strong survive and the rest go to the morgue. To strengthen your bones and muscles to withstand the rigors of a real fight, your program must include progressive resistance (weight training) and calisthenics. You will also need a stretching program designed to loosen up every muscle group. You can't kick, punch, ground fight, or otherwise execute the necessary body mechanics if you're "tight" or inflexible. Stretching on a regular basis will also increase the muscles' range of motion, improve circulation, reduce the possibility of injury, and relieve daily stress.

The final component of physical fitness is proper body composition: simply, the ratio of fat to lean body tissue. Your diet and training regimen will affect your level or percentage of body fat significantly. A sensible and consistent exercise program accompanied by a healthy and balanced diet will facilitate proper body composition. Do not neglect this important aspect of physical fitness.

Weapon and Technique Mastery

You won't stand a chance against a vicious assailant if you don't master the weapons and tools of fighting. In CFA, we teach our students both armed and unarmed methods of combat. Unarmed fighting requires that you master a complete arsenal of natural body weapons and techniques. In conjunction, you must also learn the various stances, hand positioning, footwork, body mechanics, defensive structure, locks, chokes, and various holds. Keep in mind that something as simple as a basic punch will actually require hundreds of hours to perfect.

Range proficiency is another important aspect of weapon and technique mastery. Briefly, range proficiency is the ability to fight effectively in all three ranges of unarmed fighting. Although punching range tools are emphasized in CFA, kicking and grappling ranges cannot be neglected. Our kicking range tools consist of deceptive and powerful low-line kicks. Grappling range tools include head-butts, elbows, knees, foot stomps, biting, tearing, gouging, and crushing tactics.

Although CFA focuses on striking, we also teach our students a myriad of chokes, locks, and holds that can be used in a ground fight. While such grappling range submission techniques are not the most preferred methods of dealing with a ground fighting situation, they must be studied for the following six reasons: (1) level of force - many ground fighting situations do not justify the use of deadly force. In such instances, you must apply various non-lethal submission holds, (2) nature of the beast - in order to escape any choke, lock or hold, you must first know how to apply them yourself, (3) occupational requirement- some professional occupations (police, security, etc.) require that you possess a working knowledge of various submission techniques, (4) subduing a friend or relative - in many cases it is best to restrain and control a friend or relative with a submission hold instead of striking him with a natural body weapon, (5) anatomical orientation - practicing various chokes, locks and holds will help you develop a strong orientation of the human anatomy, and (6) refutation requirement - finally, if you are going to criticize the combative limitations of any submission hold, you better be sure that you can perform it yourself.

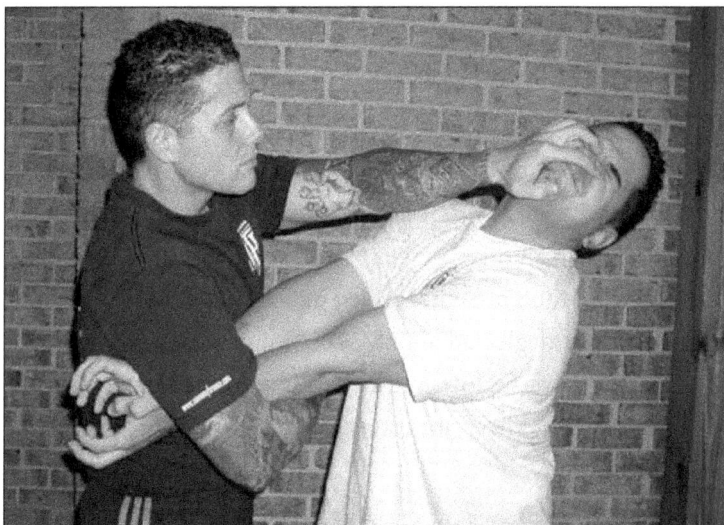

Contemporary Fighting Arts is more than a self defense system, its a one-of-a-kind martial arts style geared for real world self defense.

Defensive tools and skills are also taught. Our defensive structure is efficient, uncomplicated, and impenetrable. It provides the fighter maximum protection while allowing complete freedom of choice for acquiring offensive control. Our defensive structure is based on distance, parrying, blocking, evading, mobility, and stance structure.

Simplicity is always the key.

Students are also instructed in specific methods of armed fighting. For example, CFA provides instruction about firearms for personal and household protection. We provide specific guidelines for handgun purchasing, operation, nomenclature, proper caliber, shooting fundamentals, cleaning, and safe storage. Our firearm program also focuses on owner responsibility and the legal ramifications regarding the use of deadly force.

CFA's weapons program also consists of natural body weapons, knives and edged weapons, single and double stick, makeshift weaponry, the side-handle baton, and oleoresin capsicum (OC) spray.

Combat Attributes

Your offensive and defensive tools are useless unless they are used strategically. For any tool or technique to be effective in a real fight, it must be accompanied by specific attributes. Attributes are qualities that enhance a particular tool, technique, or maneuver. Some examples include speed, power, timing, coordination, accuracy, non-telegraphic movement, balance, and target orientation.

CFA also has a wide variety of training drills and methodologies designed to develop and sharpen these combat attributes. For example, our students learn to ground fight while blindfolded, spar with one arm tied down, and fight while handcuffed.

Reality is the key. For example, in class students participate in full-contact exercises against fully padded assailants, and real weapon disarms are rehearsed and analyzed in a variety of dangerous scenarios. Students also train with a large variety of equipment, including heavy bags, double-end bags, uppercut bags, pummel bags, focus mitts, striking shields, mirrors, rattan sticks, foam and plastic bats, kicking pads, knife drones, trigger-sensitive (mock) guns, boxing and digit gloves, full-body armor, and hundreds of different environmental props.

There are more than two hundred unique training methodologies used in Contemporary Fighting Arts. Each one is scientifically designed to prepare students for the hard-core realities of real world combat. There are also three specific training methodologies used to develop and sharpen the fundamental attributes and skills of armed and unarmed fighting, including proficiency training, conditioning training, and street training.

CFA has a several unique military combat training programs. Our mission is to provide today's modern soldier with the knowledge, skills and attitude necessary to survive a wide variety of real world combat scenarios. Our military program is designed to provide the modern soldier with the safest and most effective skills and tactics to control and decentralize armed and unarmed enemies.

Proficiency training can be used for both armed and unarmed skills. When conducted properly, proficiency training develops speed, power, accuracy, non-telegraphic movement, balance, and general psychomotor skill. The training objective is to sharpen one specific body weapon, maneuver, or technique at a time by executing it over and over for a prescribed number of repetitions. Each time the technique or maneuver is executed with "clean" form at various speeds. Movements are also performed with the eyes closed to develop a kinesthetic "feel" for the action. Proficiency training can be accomplished through the use of various types of equipment, including the heavy bag, double-end bag, focus mitts, training knives, real and mock pistols, striking shields, shin and knee guards, foam and plastic bats, mannequin heads, and so on.

Conditioning training develops endurance, fluidity, rhythm, distancing, timing, speed, footwork, and balance. In most cases, this type of training requires the student to deliver a variety of fighting combinations for three- or four-minute rounds separated by 30-second breaks. Like proficiency training, this type of training can also be performed at various speeds. A good workout consists of at least five rounds. Conditioning training can be performed on the bags with full-contact sparring gear, rubber training knives, focus mitts, kicking shields, and shin guards, or against imaginary assailants in shadow fighting.

Conditioning training is not necessarily limited to just three- or four-minute rounds. For example, CFA's ground fighting training can last as long as 30 minutes. The bottom line is that it all depends on what you are training for.

Street training is the final preparation for the real thing. Since many violent altercations are explosive, lasting an average of 20 seconds, you must prepare for this possible scenario. This means delivering explosive and powerful compound attacks with vicious intent for approximately 20 seconds, resting one minute, and then repeating the process.

Street training prepares you for the stress and immediate fatigue of a real fight. It also develops speed, power, explosiveness, target selection and recognition, timing, footwork, pacing, and breath control. You should practice this methodology in different lighting, on different terrains, and in different environmental settings. You can use different types of training equipment as well. For example, you can prepare yourself for multiple assailants by having your training partners attack you with focus mitts from a variety of angles, ranges, and target postures. For 20 seconds, go after them with vicious low-line kicks, powerful punches, and devastating strikes.

When all is said and done, the physical component creates a fighter who is physically fit and armed with a lethal arsenal of tools, techniques, and weapons that can be deployed with destructive results.

The Mental Component

The mental component of CFA focuses on the cerebral aspects of a fighter, developing killer instinct, strategic/tactical awareness, analysis and integration skills, philosophy, and cognitive skills.

The Killer Instinct

Deep within each of us is a cold and deadly primal power known as the "killer instinct." The killer instinct is a vicious combat mentality that surges to your consciousness and turns you into a fierce fighter who is free of fear, anger, and apprehension. If you want to survive the horrifying dynamics of real criminal violence, you must cultivate and utilize this instinctive killer mentality.

There are 14 characteristics of CFA's killer instinct. They are: (1) clear and lucid thinking, (2) heightened situational awareness, (3) adrenaline surge, (4) mobilized body, (5) psychomotor control, (6) absence of distraction, (7) tunnel vision, (8) fearless mind-set, (9) tactical implementation, (10) the lack of emotion, (11) breath control, (12) pseudospeciation, (13) viciousness, and (14) pain tolerance.

Visualization and crisis rehearsal are just two techniques used to develop, refine, and channel this extraordinary source of strength and energy so that it can be used to its full potential.

Strategic/Tactical Awareness

Strategy is the bedrock of preparedness. In CFA, there are three unique categories of strategic awareness that will diminish the likelihood of criminal victimization. They are criminal awareness, situational awareness, and self-awareness. When developed, these essential skills prepare you to assess a wide variety of threats instantaneously and accurately. Once you've made a proper threat assessment, you will be able to choose one of the following five self-defense options: comply, escape, de-escalate, assert, or fight back.

CFA also teaches students to assess a variety of other important factors, including the assailant's demeanor, intent, range, positioning and weapon capability, as well as such environmental issues as escape routes, barriers, terrain, and makeshift weaponry. In addition to assessment skills, CFA also teaches students how to enhance perception and observation skills.

Analysis and Integration Skills

The analytical process is intricately linked to understanding how to defend yourself in any threatening situation. If you want to be the best, every aspect of fighting and personal protection must be dissected. Every strategy, tactic, movement, and concept must be broken down to its atomic parts. The three planes (physical, mental, spiritual) of self-defense must be unified scientifically through arduous practice and constant exploration.

CFA's most advanced practitioners have sound insight and understanding of a wide range of sciences and disciplines. They include human anatomy, kinesiology, criminal justice, sociology, kinesics, proxemics, combat physics, emergency medicine, crisis management, histrionics, police and military science, the psychology of aggression, and the role of archetypes.

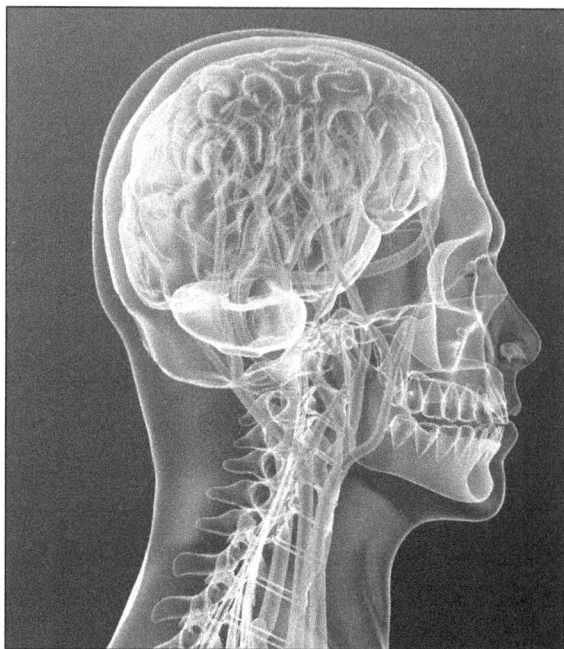

CFA's mental component focuses on the cognitive development of a fighter, including strategic/tactical awareness, analysis and integration, cognitive skills, the killer instinct, and philosophy.

Analytical exercises are also a regular part of CFA training. For example, we conduct problem-solving sessions involving particular assailants attacking in defined environments. We move hypothetical attackers through various ranges to provide insight into tactical solutions. We scrutinize different methods of attack for their general utility in combat. We also discuss the legal ramifications of self-defense on a frequent basis.

In addition to problem-solving sessions, students are slowly exposed to concepts of integration and modification. Oral and written examinations are given to measure intellectual accomplishment. Unlike traditional systems, CFA does not use colored belts or sashes to identify the student's level of proficiency.

Philosophy

Philosophical resolution is essential to a fighter's mental confidence and clarity. Anyone learning the art of war must find the ultimate answers to questions concerning the use of violence in defense of himself or others. To advance to the highest levels of combat awareness, you must find clear and lucid answers to such provocative questions as could you take the life of another, what are your fears, who are you, why are you interested in studying Contemporary Fighting Arts, why are you reading this book, and what is good and what is evil? If you haven't begun the quest to

Developing a deadly capability to protect yourself carries tremendous moral and social responsibility. It also involves the risk of civil liability and criminal jeopardy. There is an interesting irony facing most martial artists or self-defense experts. The more highly trained, knowledgeable, and skilled you are in firearms, knives, unarmed combat tactics, martial arts, and other self-defense skills, the higher the standards of care you must follow when protecting yourself and others.

formulate these important questions and answers, then take a break. It's time to figure out just why you want to know the laws and rules of destruction.

Cognitive Combat Skills

Cognitive combat exercises are also important for improving one's fighting skills. CFA uses visualization and crisis rehearsal scenarios to improve general body mechanics, tools and techniques, and maneuvers, as well as tactic selection. Mental clarity, concentration, and emotional control are also developed to enhance one's ability to call upon the controlled killer instinct.

The Spiritual Component

There are many tough fighters out there. In fact, they reside in every town in every country. However, most are nothing more than vicious animals that lack self-mastery. And self-mastery is what separates the true warrior from the eternal novice.

I am not referring to religious precepts or beliefs when I speak of CFA's spiritual component. Unlike most martial arts, CFA does not merge religion into its spiritual aspect. Religion is a very personal and private matter and should never, be incorporated into any fighting system.

CFA's spiritual component is not something that is taught or studied. Rather, it is that which transcends the physical and mental aspects of being and reality. There is a deeper part of each of us that is a tremendous source of truth and accomplishment.

In CFA, the spiritual component is something that is slowly and progressively acquired. During the challenging quest of combat training, one begins to tap the higher qualities of human nature. Those elements of our being that inherently enable us to know right from wrong and good from evil. As we slowly develop this aspect of our total self, we begin to strengthen qualities profoundly important to the "truth." Such qualities are essential to your growth through the mastery of inner peace, the clarity of your "vision," and your recognition of universal truths.

While there are many dedicated individuals who are more than qualified to teach unique philosophical and spiritual components of ancient martial arts, you must realize that such forms of combat can get you killed in a real life self-defense encounter.

One of the goals of my system is to promote virtue and moral responsibility in people who have extreme capacities for physical and mental destructiveness. The spiritual component of fighting is truly the most difficult aspect of personal growth. Yet, unlike the physical component, where the practitioner's abilities will be limited to some degree by genetics and other natural factors, the spiritual component of combat offers unlimited potential for growth and development. In the final analysis, CFA's spiritual component poses the greatest challenges for the student. It is an open-ended plane of unlimited advancement.

The 10 Best Mental Toughness Exercises

Chapter One
What is Mental Toughness?

What is Mental Toughness?

Ask ten people what it means to be mentally tough, and you will likely get ten different answers. This is because mental toughness is a vague and subjective term that is difficult to validate. In fact, no two definitions of mental toughness will ever be exact.

Therefore, for the purposes of this book, I'm going to give you my interpretation of mental toughness based on my personal experiences and observations. Essentially, mental toughness is a performance mechanism utilizing a collection of mental qualities that allows a person to cope, perform and prevail through the stress of extreme adversity.

Mental toughness is also a form of self-mastery that plays an essential role in determining optimal performance and success in combat, sports, health, and other important aspects of life. Like any skill or attribute, mental toughness is something that can be learned and developed.

Unfortunately, many people use the term mental toughness loosely. Some self-appointed experts claim that it's simply a collection of positive qualities that help a person cope with a tough situation. For example, this might include something as trivial as preparing for a midterm exam or working in a competitive business environment. Unfortunately, such a cavalier interpretation is misleading and weakens the very essence of this vital performance mechanism.

Finally, not every form of mental toughness is alike. For instance, the mental resilience necessary to survive a prisoner-of-war camp is dramatically different from than the mental strength required to endure and complete the Marathon des Sables. While the two might share similar mental toughness attributes, they are drastically different experiences, requiring dissimilar forms of training.

The Six Elements of Extreme Adversity

Genuine mental toughness is demonstrated when you are confronted with an extreme form of adversity. Examples would include, competing against a superior opponent or performing a mission critical task in a hostile and dangerous environment. Generally, extreme adversity will include most of the following six elements:

- **A degree of Danger**
- **The element of Risk**
- **The presence of Fear**
- **The possibility of Loss**
- **A challenge to your Self-confidence**
- **The experience of Pain (emotional or physical)**

In fact, genuine mental strength requires you to activate every fiber of your being (mentally, emotionally, physically, and spiritually). It's no wonder mental toughness is readily identified with elite military units, like the United States Navy SEALS. These elite warriors are the foundation of Naval Special Warfare combat forces. They are considered the best of the best because they are trained to conduct a wide range of Special Operations missions in all types of extreme climates and hostile environments, including the sea, air, and land.

Pictured here, a Navy Special Warfare Trident insignia worn exclusively by U.S. Navy SEALs.

Physical and Psychological Adversity

Extreme adversity can materialize in one of two forms: physical or psychological. Physical adversity requires you to cope and perform during a physically stressful event or circumstance. For example, physical adversity can be a high-risk self-defense situation requiring you to defend against a physically superior adversary in the street. Or, it could be something less menacing like a competitive wrestling match against a powerful and determined opponent. Both of these examples, however, will still require a substantial amount of mental toughness to cope and perform under these circumstances.

Conversely, psychological adversity requires you to cope and perform during a psychologically stressful event or circumstance. For example, it might require you to withstand the psychological torment of a bully or the relentless taunting of a drill sergeant.

Many traditional occupations might also expose you to various forms of psychological adversity. For example, consider a police officer who must confront and diffuse a verbally abusive crowd or a professional athlete who is regularly insulted by overzealous spectators.

Both of these examples require a certain degree of mental toughness to cope and perform when faced with the stress of adversity. Finally, physical and psychological adversity are not mutually exclusive. More often than not, they are experienced at the same time.

```
┌─────────────────────┐
│      Adversity      │
└─────────────────────┘
```

┌──────────────┐   ┌────────────────────┐
│   Physical   │   │   Psychological   │
└──────────────┘   └────────────────────┘

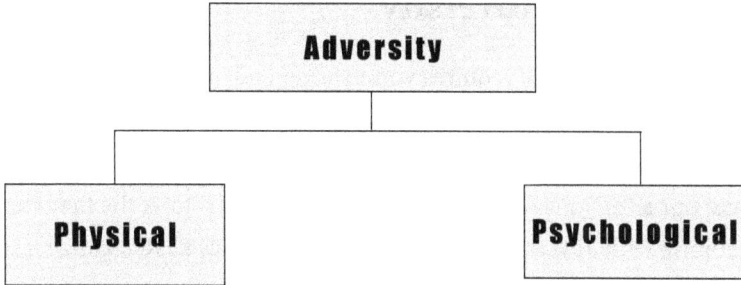

Adversity can be divided into two categories: physical and psychological.

Three Objectives of Mental Toughness

Regardless of your occupation, profession or personal goals, mental toughness has three primary objectives. They include the following:

1. To **cope** with adversity.
2. To **perform** during adversity.
3. To **prevail** from adversity.

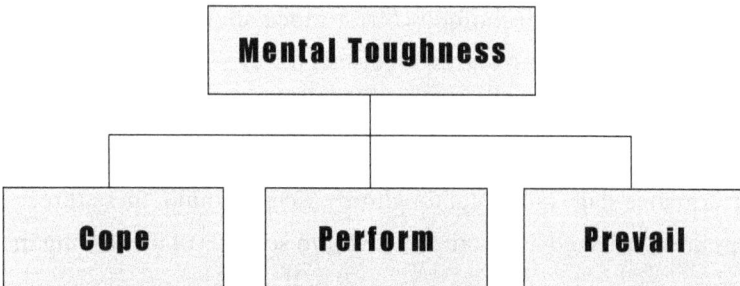

┌─────────────────────┐
│ Mental Toughness   │
└─────────────────────┘

┌──────────┐   ┌──────────┐   ┌──────────┐
│   Cope   │   │ Perform │   │ Prevail │
└──────────┘   └──────────┘   └──────────┘

The three primary objectives of mental toughness is to cope, perform, and prevail during adversity.

Coping with Adversity

Mental toughness requires you to accept adverse circumstances. This is counter-intuitive for most people because we are born with a natural instinct to avoid conflict and discomfort. In fact, we often make our situations worse by avoiding them. Therefore, the first step to coping with adversity is to identify and embrace it. Recognize it for what it is - a legitimate obstacle to your goal.

Effectively coping with adversity also means you must immediately manage and control the stress that comes with it. This is critical because it determines whether or not you'll be able to perform at the right moment.

Stress is simply the physiological and psychological arousal caused by a stressor. A stressor is any activity, situation, circumstance, event, experience, or condition that causes a person to experience either physical or mental anxiety. Stressors come in many different forms (mental, physical and emotional), and they can wreck havoc on anyone who is not prepared to handle them.

The first step to manage stress is to observe and acknowledge it. Next, you must immediately prohibit it from affecting your mind and body. You can accomplish this by using a wide range of coping skills, including meditation, mental visualization, positive self-talk, and controlled breathing techniques. Stress inoculation techniques can also be used to minimize stressful events (more will be discussed in a later chapter).

Finally, you must redirect your thoughts and actions to the performance stage of mental toughness. Keep in mind, these three steps are conducted and completed within seconds of identifying the stressor.

Performing in the Face of Adversity

Once you have confronted and accepted adversity and managed the stress associated with it, it's time to take action! Performing under the pressure of adversity will require that your course of action meet three essential requirements: efficiency, effectiveness, and safety.

- **Efficiency** - you course of action is performed in the quickest and most economical fashion.

- **Effectiveness** - your course of action achieves your goal or objective.

- **Safety** - you course of action is performed with the least possible amount of risk or danger.

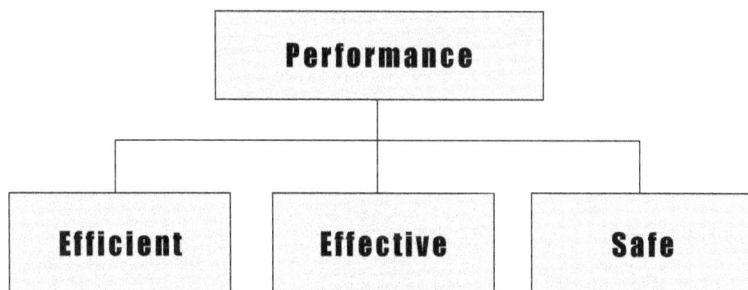

When performing in the face of adversity, your actions must fulfill three essential requirements: efficiency, effectiveness and safety.

Prevailing in the Face of Adversity

It's not enough to survive through adversity. For example, if you're a police officer engaged in a deadly firefight with the criminal, your ultimate goal is to prevail from the dangerous encounter. Similarly, if you are a soldier, your goal might entail defeating a hostile enemy in order to achieve the objectives of your mission. The same concept applies to competitors and athletes. On the field or in the ring, your goal is plain and simple - beat your opponent and win!

The 10 Best Mental Toughness Exercises

Chapter Two
Mental Toughness Characteristics

Mental Toughness Attributes

Now that you have a general understanding of mental toughness, it's time to delve deeper into this invaluable source of mind power. Mental toughness consists of several interrelated elements know as attributes. Essentially, this collection of attributes can either be reactive or proactive.

A reactive attribute is a quality that allows you to cope and perform during the immediate stress and pressure of adversity. While a proactive attribute is used to maintain optimum performance under less stressful conditions. Both types of attributes serve as the essential building blocks of mental toughness.

The Mental Toughness Package

During my 30+ years of teaching the combat sciences to law enforcement, military personnel, athletes and people of all backgrounds, I have discovered that a complete mental toughness package consists of the following core attributes.

- Instrumental Aggression
- Assertiveness
- Resilience
- Self-Confidence
- Self-Discipline
- Awareness
- Attention Control
- Philosophical Resolution
- Responsibility
- Courage

What About the Killer Instinct?

Please don't confuse mental toughness with its cousin the killer instinct. While both have similar attributes, mental toughness is the stable internal climate that nourishes and ultimately brings about the killer instinct.

The killer instinct is an emotionless, primal mindset that surges to your conscious mind and transforms you into a vicious combatant. Deep within every person is a deadly primal power, a virtuous killer instinct that is cold, calculated, and primed for destruction.

The killer instinct is also a reservoir of energy and strength. It can channel your destructiveness by producing a mental wellspring of cold, destructive energy. If necessary, it fuels the determination to battle until the very end.

Nature or Nurture?

Are mental toughness attributes learned or instinctual? This question has perplexed psychologists and coaches for decades, creating a debate over the nature theory and the nurture theory.

Advocates of the nature theory believe that mental toughness is innately linked to biological, genetic and physiological factors. Built into the machine if you will. On the other hand, advocates of the nurture theory believe that mental toughness is learned from your environment and various other external factors.

The debate between these two schools of thought has gone on for some time and will most likely continue. I strongly believe that mental toughness is a combination of both nature and nurture. The raw instinct for mental toughness was manifested from the beginning of man's existence. It was a vital factor in his survival against nature's brutality, including the threat of other aggressors like himself. His adaption to adversity, accompanied with his unique problem solving abilities seem to be a combination of both genetic factors and environmental influences. Where one influence leaves off and the other picks up is impossible to say.

However, the important point is that mental toughness can be learned and developed. The first step, however, is to recognize and understand its core attributes. Only then can mental toughness be fully developed, and ultimately honed to maximize your performance during critical situations.

Now, let's take a closer look at the individual components of mental toughness. We will start with Instrumental aggression.

Instrumental Aggression

"Aggressive fighting for the right is the noblest sport the world affords."

-Theodore Roosevelt

For many people, the concept of aggression immediately conjures up images of senseless and overt acts of violence directed against another individual. There are others who believe that human aggression is the root of all evil and the primary cause of social conflict and global warfare.

However, human aggression is a necessary behavior trait that has ensured the survival of our species, and it's also a vital component of mental toughness. Essentially, there are two distinct categories of aggression: instrumental and reactive.

Instrumental aggression - purposeful and controlled aggressive action designed to help achieve a particular objective or goal. A police officer arresting a criminal suspect or a bouncer physically ejecting a belligerent patron from a bar, are good examples.

Reactive aggression - impulsive and emotionally charged aggressive action that is provoked by an external source. For example, a woman who slaps a man for insulting her, is clearly demonstrating reactive aggression. A road rage incident is also another good example of reactive aggression.

Mental toughness regularly requires the application of instrumental aggression. As a matter of fact, I define instrumental aggression as purposeful and controlled violence directed to a specific person while maintaining both strategic and tactical objectives.

Instrumental aggression is particularly important for occupations and activities that require you to administer physical force, such as military service, police work, private security, and self-defense. Full-contact sports like boxing, mixed martial arts, kick boxing, wrestling, football, rugby, lacrosse, roller derby, and ice hockey will also benefit from controlled aggression.

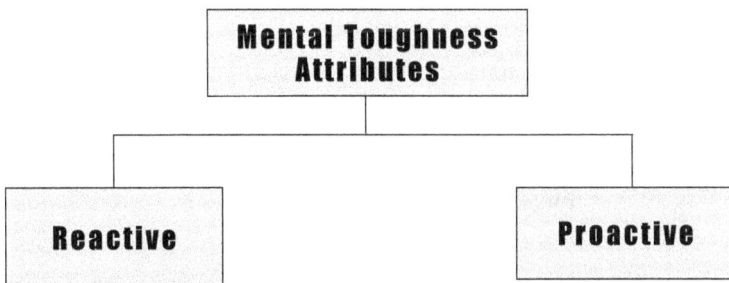

There are two different types of attributes that comprise mental toughness: reactive and proactive

Assertiveness

*"Take the place and attitude to which you see your
unquestionable right, and all men acquiesce."*

– Emerson

Just about every sporting event or high-risk occupation involves
some form of interaction and communication between people. For
example, in sports there will be an exchange of words or behaviors
between teammates, coaches, family members, and spectators. In
high-risk occupations like police work, you might be required to
interact with a host of different people including supervisors, co-
workers, civilians, and criminals.

In order to perform at your best, you must possess a healthy
degree of assertiveness. Assertiveness is a form of behavior
characterized as a confident and positive expression of your thoughts,
feeling, and needs. On the other hand, it doesn't mean being pushy,
intrusive, confrontational, or autocratic.

Highly competitive sporting events are not won by meek
individuals. Athletes must possess healthy communication skills.
They must be able to express their goals, needs and rights to
other teammates and coaches. Failing to assert yourself with both
teammates and coaches can be problematic and self-destructive.
Actively avoiding unpleasant confrontations or suppressing or
denying your feelings can be damaging on many levels, resulting in
loss of confidence and self-respect. In addition, you might experience
feelings of powerlessness, anger, frustration, anxiousness, and
resentment. More importantly, passive communication tells others
that you are weak and not to be taken seriously.

Assertiveness skills are also critical for high-risk occupations like police and security work. As a peace officer, your job requires the discretionary use of authority accompanied by an assertive police presence. Your job often requires a definitive and confident response to troublesome people and challenging situations. Assertiveness is a healthy and essential form of communication that allows you to persuade other people to see your goals and needs without alienating or disrespecting them. As a result, you will be able to keep the lines of communication open while performing your duties with a greater level of professionalism.

Assertiveness is also a vital trait in the world of self-defense. The immutable fact is humans, by nature, take full advantage of weak and timid personalities. And it's no surprise that meek people get manipulated and exploited by shrewd and psychologically dominant individuals. Through effective communication skills, you can thwart a person's efforts to intimidate, dominate, and control you.

For example, let's say you're working late at the office, and your co-worker makes sexual advances toward you. In this instance, you would be assertive and confront him. In a firm and confident manner, you would tell him that you're not interested in his advances, and you want him to stop his offensive actions immediately. It's this confident and assertive attitude that makes you less likely to be perceived as an easy mark. Weakness and uncertainty are replaced by confidence and strength. You are seen as self-assured and purposeful and you less likely to be perceived as a victim.

Resilience

"A champion is someone who gets up when he can't."

- Jack Dempsey

Resilience is the ability to recover quickly from various forms of adversity. Essentially, it provides the mental strength to "bounce back" or "get back on your feet" and continue pursuing your goal or objective. For example, an athlete might sustain a physical injury or embarrassing performance mistake. A soldier might experience psychological trauma from war, or a police officer might experience post-traumatic stress from a deadly shootout with the criminal. As diverse as these examples might be, all of them require a substantial amount of mental resiliency to recover and get back on track.

Resiliency requires you to be adaptable. You must possess the necessary physical and mental skills to adapt to the rapidly changing circumstances of your environment. In combat, for example, factors and circumstances change like the wind. A prepared combatant knows how and when to adapt to his environment. Adaptability allows one to adjust to new or different conditions or circumstances both physically and psychologically. In the heat of combat, a soldier doesn't have the luxury of questioning change. He or she cannot overly scrutinize a particular situation. In fact, he must simply conform to the immediate demands of his predicament.

Two Types of Resilience

There are two distinct categories of mental resiliency: immediate and reflective. Let's take a look at each one.

Immediate Resilience

Immediate resilience requires you to adapt immediately to the stress you experience during a crisis or event. For example, consider a professional boxer who encounters an unexpected hook to the head during a match. To stay on his feet and avoid going "down for the count", he must immediately adapt and make the necessary adjustments to regain his equilibrium, balance, and mental composure. During his opponent's flurry of punches that follow suit, the boxer must remain focused and not fold under pressure. It's during this crisis moment, he must demonstrate the immediate resilience to bounce back and endure the pain and emotional anxiety associated with his opponent's vicious assault.

Immediate resilience is particularly important for grueling endurance sports like triathlons, marathons, ultramarathons, and extreme obstacle races. Endurance sports are about mental willpower. They require you to compete against your most formidable opponent - yourself. In order to perform well, you must possess the mental resilience to cope with the inevitable pain, fatigue, and exhaustion that comes with these types of endurance events. Immediate resilience simply gives you the mental wherewithal to push through these obstacles and win.

Reflective Resilience

Reflective resilience, on the other hand is the ability to bounce back from setbacks that involve either physical injury or mental trauma. In many ways, it's a form of picking up the pieces and rebounding from adversity. For example, a professional athlete who experiences a serious sports injury might become disheartened and question whether he has the skill and talent to pursue his journey. His despair brings him to a mental crossroad where he must summon the resilience to fight his fears and apprehensions. Reflective resilience provides the athlete with the strength and resolve to work his way back to his previous healthy state. Moreover, with serious thought and honest reflection, the athlete acquires a renewed sense of motivation and commitment.

Finally, reflective resilience is essential for individuals who experience psychological trauma from hazardous duties. Consider a soldier, who experiences the horrors of war might suffer from combat stress reaction (CSR) or a police officer who experiences a traumatic incident might develop post-traumatic stress. Reflective resilience acts as a type of mental armor that protects your psyche and helps you recover from a traumatic event.

Self-Confidence

"They can do all because they think they can."

- Vergil

Successful athletes thrive during high-pressure competition because they are confident they possess the skills and ability necessary to beat their opponents. Their self-confidence serves as an effective coping mechanism to overcome anxiety, self-doubt, intimidation, and fear during a high-performance event.

Self-confidence means having an unshakable trust in both your judgment skills and abilities. However, it should not be confused with arrogance or false bravado. In fact, you must be self-aware. You must have an accurate and realistic perspective of yourself including both your inherent strengths and weaknesses. When all is said and done, dangerous poisons like egotism, conceit and narcissism will undermine your goals by instilling a false reality.

Self-confidence can be infectious and will often have a spillover effect in team sports. For example, an athlete who believes in himself resolutely, often inspires his teammates to push past their limits during difficult circumstances. He might also energize spectators and fans to rally and cheer his team to victory. Conversely, players demonstrating low self-esteem, poor self-image and a lack of confidence can also cripple a team and bring it down to its collective knees.

Staring into the Face of Danger

Self-confidence is both a proactive and reactive tool. For example, in self-defense you need a substantial amount of self-confidence to confront a threatening attacker. Defending yourself against a violent attack requires a tremendous amount of personal faith in your skills and abilities. In this instance, you are demonstrating a reactive form of self-confidence.

Self-confidence can also be proactive. For instance, when walking in public, avoid showing signs of weakness and insecurity. Instead, keep your head up and carry yourself with confidence and purpose. When conversing with people, demonstrate strength and confidence by maintaining direct eye contact. As trivial as they may seem, these proactive forms of self-confidence are vital for your personal safety.

Self-Discipline

"He who conquers others is strong; he who conquers himself is mighty."

–Lao Tse

Self-discipline is considered the single most important trait required to achieve personal excellence. As a matter of fact, it's self-discipline that separates the novice from the expert and the highly accomplished person from the underachiever. Self-discipline is the ability to work methodically and consistently toward a personal goal until it is achieved. In some instances, it might require you to work tirelessly day after day, week after week, and month after month until your objective is actualized.

Self-discipline requires you to control and manage your impulses, emotions and desires so you can effectively pursue and ultimately reach your goals. It means having the self-control to ignore the deleterious temptations of instant gratification, in favor of acquiring a more meaningful and sometimes arduous goal.

Self-discipline does not mean living your life like an ascetic monk or denying yourself worldly pleasures. It doesn't mean limiting or restricting your lifestyle or abstaining from enjoyable things. Rather, self-discipline means focusing your mind exclusively on a goal and directing all of your energy until you achieve your objective.

Self-discipline also means controlling your mind and body with positive and purposeful choices, instead of negative emotions, bad habits, and external influences. Simply put, self-discipline allows you to achieve your goals in a very efficient and effective manner.

The Three Steps of Self-Discipline

Self-discipline is not just a trait, it's also a skill that can be learned. It requires you to take three simple yet effective steps. First, you must make a specific decision. Second, you must take the necessary action for that decision. Third, you must follow-through with the proper course of action (despite the obstacles that come with it) until you achieve your goal or objective.

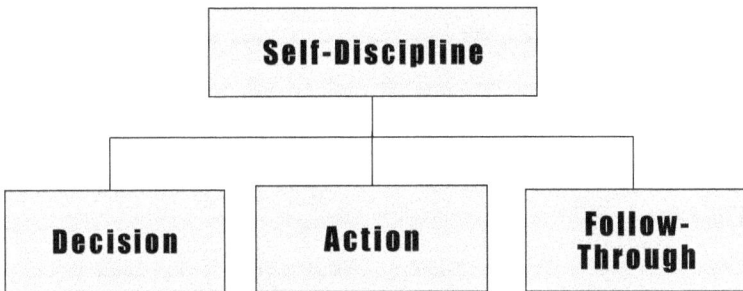

```
            ┌─────────────────────┐
            │   Self-Discipline   │
            └─────────────────────┘
    ┌───────────────┬───────────────┐
┌─────────┐   ┌─────────┐   ┌─────────┐
│Decision │   │ Action  │   │ Follow- │
│         │   │         │   │ Through │
└─────────┘   └─────────┘   └─────────┘
```

Self-discipline is a relatively simple three stage process.

Other Benefits of Self-Discipline

There are many other benefits of self-discipline, here are a few.

• Self-discipline increases your self-confidence.

• Self-discipline improves your creativity and imagination.

• Self-discipline sharpens and refines analytical thinking.

• Self discipline promotes leadership skills.

• Self-discipline generates respect from other people.

• Self-discipline gives you a greater passion for life.

Self-Discipline Exercises:

1.In your own words, briefly describe what self-discipline means
to you.

_____

_____

_____

_____

_____

_____

_____

2. Describe the most self-disciplined person you know and
explain his or her success.

_____

_____

_____

_____

_____

_____

_____

3. Describe the least self-disciplined person you know and
explain his or her failures.

_____

_____

_____

_____

_____

_____

_____

_____

4. Name three aspects of your life that are in desperate need of self-discipline.

_____

_____

_____

_____

_____

_____

_____

_____

_____

5. Briefly describe three problems you are currently experiencing due to a lack of self-discipline.

_____

_____

_____

_____

_____

_____

_____

_____

_____

6. Describe several benefits you will acquire from developing self-discipline.

_____

_____

_____

_____

_____

_____

_____

_____

Awareness

"The ultimate value of life depends upon awareness and the power of contemplation rather than upon mere survival."

-Aristotle

Your awareness or perception of people, places, actions, and objects is a vital component of mental toughness. In fact, peak performance in every activity or endeavor can only be achieved through the proper awareness skills. Awareness gives you the ability to respond rapidly and successfully to a wide variety of stressful situations and circumstances. In addition, it offers the necessary introspection to identify which aspects of yourself create obstacles that prevent you from achieving your goals.

Your Perception Matters

Awareness is directly linked to your perceptions. Perception is the interpretation of information acquired through one's senses when faced with a stressful or dangerous situation. You gather information through your five senses. Your eyes, ears, nose, and senses of touch and taste will provide a wealth of vital information about your environment. With adequate training, your senses can be sharpened, and your powers of observation enhanced.

The ability to process information varies from person to person. In fact, two people who witness the same event are likely to report it differently. This is referred to as "individual perception." In part, previous experiences can determine the manner in which a person will interpret stimuli. When it comes to achieving peak performance in combat and athletics, you must attempt to remove preconceived notions, assumptions, and biases that may lead to dangerously incorrect conclusions or oversights. These false reactions form barriers to your ability to grasp reality.

Two Types of Awareness

There are two types of awareness that are directly linked to mental toughness. They are: *situational* and *self-awareness*. Let's start by taking a look at situational awareness.

Situational Awareness

Situational awareness is total alertness, presence, and focus on virtually everything in your immediate surroundings. For example, if you are a soldier, police officer or security agent, you must train your senses to detect and assess the people, places, objects, and actions that can pose a danger to you. Do not think of situational awareness simply in terms of the five customary senses of sight, sound, smell, taste, and touch. In addition, the very real powers of instinct and intuition must also be developed and eventually relied upon.

Self-defense clearly illustrates this point. For example, a vagrant congregating by your car, the stranger lingering in your apartment hallway, two men following you in a deserted parking lot, the stray dog ambling toward you in the park, a large limb hanging precariously from a tree... these are all obvious examples of persons, places, and objects that pose a threat to you.

Situational awareness also diminishes the potency of the criminal's favorite weapon - the element of surprise. Your ability to foresee and detect danger will diminish his ability to stalk you, or lie in wait in ambush zones. In addition to enhancing your ability to detect, avoid, and strategically neutralize ambush zones, situational awareness allows you to detect and avoid threats and dangers not necessarily predicated on the element of surprise. Some situations afford potential victims the luxury of seeing trouble coming. Nonetheless, it's remarkable how many people fail to heed obvious signs of danger because of poor awareness skills. They overlook the signals - belligerence, furtiveness, hostility, restlessness - so often manifested by criminal attackers. They neglect the opportunity to cross the street long before the shoulder-to-shoulder encounter with a pack of young toughs moving up the sidewalk. Once it's too late to avoid the confrontation, a whole new range of principles comes quickly into play.

How to Sharpen Your Senses

Your five senses (sight, smell, touch, sound, and taste) can be sharpened through a variety of exercises designed to develop both raw detection and learned identification abilities.

For example, sit on a park bench for a given period of time and catalog the various objects and actions your five senses detect, then list the possible sources of the sensory data. With sufficient practice, you will make significant progress from being unable to detect a particular sound or smell to not only detecting it quickly and accurately, but also identifying its source. Remember that sensory development increases as these exercises are performed in different environmental settings.

Trust Your Instincts

Situational awareness also means trusting your instincts. Learn to rely on your innate ability to know or sense something without the use of rational thought. In many circumstances, immediate cognition will provide you with the necessary time to respond to a challenging or threatening situation. In some situations, going with your "gut" reaction can be just what is called for. Remember, when something doesn't seem right, or the objective data doesn't add up, then chances are something is wrong.

Emotional Recognition Exercise

The objective of this exercise is to sharpen your ability to recognize and identify various emotional states in people. To perform the exercise, spend approximately 20 minutes in a busy public place (i.e., train station, bus stop, sporting event, courtroom, shopping mall, emergency room, airport, etc.), and observe people's emotional states. Pay close attention to their posture, voice, demeanor, hand movements, and facial expressions. Note them in writing.

Combat Situational Awareness Exercises

1. If your occupation requires you to work in potentially dangerous or hostile environments, detect at least ten different ambush zones at your workplace and write them down. Don't pick the obvious ones. It's your life; learn to think like the bad guy.

2. Detect ten different ambush zones in front of your home. If you didn't find ten, you didn't look hard enough.

3. Over the next ten days do not allow yourself to be taken by surprise -by anyone! Every time it happens, record the circumstances: who, what, when, how, where, and why.

4. When you watch television, go to the movies, look at pictures, read books, or play video games, note ambush zones that have not occurred to you in your other assessments. Note them in writing.

5. Visualize five different settings. They can be friendly and familiar like your backyard, or hostile and strange. Write down the things that you have mentally noted in these visualized settings.

6. When observing people in public places, try to identify at least five places on their body where they could be concealing a weapon.

Self-Awareness

Self-awareness has been the subject of philosophers and mystics for centuries. Socrates said, "Know thyself." He believed self-knowledge to be essential to the attainment of true virtue. Self-awareness empowers athletes by giving them invaluable information about their strengths, weaknesses, attitudes, motivations, and beliefs.

The key to making positive changes in your behavior and ultimately improving your performance is first to understand yourself in relation to your sport. Self-awareness gives both athletes and warriors the experiential knowledge to control his or her performance during highly stressful events.

Self-awareness involves the harmonious integration of your mind and body to gain full-control of any high-pressure performance situation. It allows you to read, interpret, and understand what your body is telling you. As a result, you remain calm, focused, and in complete control of your emotions when experiencing both performance success and failures.

Moreover, self-awareness helps you mentally recall, imprint, and hopefully replicate the positive experiences of an ideal performance state. Conversely, it also helps you recognize, identify and avoid the negative and unproductive elements that come with a poor performance.

Different Forms of Sports Performance Awareness

- The athlete is focused exclusively on the immediate performance task.

- The athlete makes accurate assessments and adjustments during performance.

- The athlete recognizes his or her limitations while performing.

- The athlete understands the stressors that cause poor performance.

- The athlete is able to control his emotions during performance.

Self-Awareness Questions for Sports Performance

The following questions were designed to start you thinking in the important process of self-awareness. Use them to form an overall personal profile of yourself.

1. What essential qualities do you bring to your sport?
2. What essential qualities do you bring to your team?
3. What separates you from other athletes in your field?
4. What are your feelings (both positive and negative) about your sport?
5. What does performance success mean to you? Give examples.
6. What does performance failure mean to you? Give examples.
7. Exactly how do you feel when you perform at your best?
8. What enables you to perform at your best?
9. What contributes to your performance failures?
10. Exactly how do you feel when you perform poorly?

Self-Awareness for Combat

Self-awareness is also a critical component of combat training and self-defense. For example, what aspects of yourself provoke violence and which, if any, would promote a proper reaction in defense against a threat of violence to you or others? Let's look at certain aspects important to self-protection and ask ourselves a few tough questions.

Physical Attributes

What are your physical strengths and weaknesses? Are you overweight or underweight? Is your body language and the manner in which you carry yourself more likely to provoke or deter a violent attack? Do you have any training in self-defense? Are you fit or out of shape? Do you have the skill to disarm a knife-wielding attacker? Do you smoke or drink excessively? Are you skilled with firearms or edged weapons?

Mental Attributes

What are your mental strengths and weaknesses? Are you an optimist or pessimist? Can you summon up courage and confidence even when you are feeling fearful or insecure? How do you handle stress? Do you panic or frighten easily? Do you have any phobias? What are your fears? Do you think well on your feet?

Communication Skills

What are your strengths and weaknesses in expressing yourself with words? Are you likely to aggravate or diffuse a hostile situation? Are your words congruent with your tone of voice? Can you communicate adequately under stressful situations, or do you become nonplused?

Personality Traits

What type of person are you? Are you passive or aggressive? Are you opinionated and argumentative or open-minded and deliberative? Are you fiery, loud, and boisterous, or quiet, subdued, and calm? Are you quick to anger? Do you harbor grudges? Are there sensitive issues or remarks that may cause you to lose your temper?

Gender and Age

What are the different types of violent crimes that are directed toward you because of your sex? Women are much more likely than men to be raped or abused by their spouses. On the other hand, males are more likely than females to be victims of homicides. Is your age an open invitation for an attack? Children are more likely to be molested or kidnapped than adults, and older adults are weaker and more vulnerable to attack than middle-aged people.

Occupation

Does the nature of your occupation make you or your family vulnerable to different forms of criminal violence? Are you involved with the military or law enforcement? Are you a celebrity? Do you have diplomatic or political connections? Do you control large sums of money or valuable drugs? Does your political affiliation make you or your family a likely target for kidnapping and terrorism?

Income Level

What types of crime are directed toward you because of your income level? Self awareness means knowing and understanding yourself. This includes aspects of yourself which may provoke criminal violence and which will promote a proper and strong reaction to an attack. Are you wealthy, comfortable, or poor? Does your income level make you and your family vulnerable to kidnapping for ransom? Or does your financial situation force you and your family to live in poor neighborhoods that invite violent crime? Are you wealthy and flashy with outward evidence of this wealth?

Self-Awareness Exercises

The following questions will help you recognize the traits that provoke and/or prevent a violent attack.

- Think of five physical and five mental weaknesses that would inhibit your survival in a self-defense situation.

- Recall a very stressful situation. How did you react? How did you feel? Were you angry? Did you lose control? Were you calm, notwithstanding the pressure?

- Ask a close friend or your spouse to evaluate your

- communication skills in a variety of situations with other people. Are you open and receptive, rude or polite, emphatic and expressive, or reserved and withdrawn? Do not react defensively to the critique you receive, even if you don't agree.

- Look into the mirror and conjure up the following mental and emotional states, carefully noting your facial expressions as they arise: anger, happiness, sadness, depression, surprise, and fear.

- Go back to the preceding exercise and focus on anger. Pay close attention to your facial expressions and other physiological manifestations. What do you see?

- Think of three forms of violent crime that you may be subject to because of your occupation.

- Think of three forms of violent crime that you may be subject to because of your gender.

- To gain a better understanding of yourself, complete the following four exercises. Be frank and truthful.

- Do you believe you could take the life of another human being?

- List four of your greatest fears.

- What steps might you take to eliminate or diminish those fears?

- Name three issues, topics, comments, or situations that would provoke you to lose your temper.

Attention Control

"The field of consciousness is tiny. It accepts only one problem at a time. Get into a fist fight, put your mind on the strategy of the fight, and you will not feel the other fellows punches."

- Saint-Exupéry

Earlier, I discussed situational awareness and its importance for mental toughness. Situational awareness provides the raw data of your immediate surroundings, while attention control is the ability to select what stimuli to pay attention to and what to ignore. Attention control is actually a combination of two mental skills: *selective attention* and *concentration.*

Selective attention is the ability to filter out and ignore the unnecessary sights, sounds, sensations, thoughts, and emotions and focus exclusively on stimuli that is pertinent to your goal or objective. Simply put, it means selecting and discriminating the valuable data that is critically important to your task, from a considerable amount of junk. Concentration, on the other hand, is the ability to sustain attention over a specific period of time.

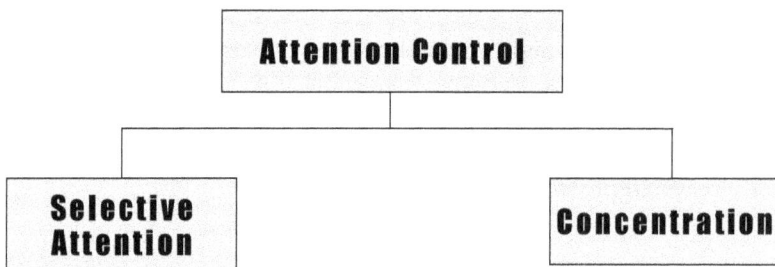

Attention control is a combination of both Selective Attention and Concentration.

Concentration Shifting

Both warriors and athletes are required to shift their attention constantly during critical performance moments. At any given time, they might be required to shift their focus from internal to external or broad to narrow. For example, during a professional fight, a mixed martial artist must first focus his attention internally by develop a winning strategy predicated on his opponent's apparent strengths and weaknesses. Then, he shifts his attention to external factors like the opponent's range, movement, angle of attack, and punch trajectory. Finally, he narrows his focus even further by delivering a precisely timed knockout counter strike.

Two Sources of Distraction

Concentration requires a unified mind that is free from all types of distractions and fully focused on the immediate situation. Distractions are derived from one of two sources. The first is eternal, where in your mind wanders off or panics prior to or during a stressful situation.

The second is external when outside elements force your mind to lose focus. For example, when your opponent attempts to verbally "psych you out" for example. Or when you become physically injured during a dangerous crisis situation. Environmental conditions such as weather, lighting, terrain, and noise can also create external distractions.

For this reason, I teach my students how to avoid being distracted by the opponent during the pre-contact stages of a self-defense altercation. For example, they are taught to disregard such things as psych-out techniques, threatening gestures, eye movements, abusive language, and drastic fluctuations in voice including tone, pitch, tempo, and volume.

The 10 Best Mental Toughness Exercises

Regardless of the source, distractions must be ignored and ultimately eliminated from your consciousness if you are to achieve peak performance in any endeavor.

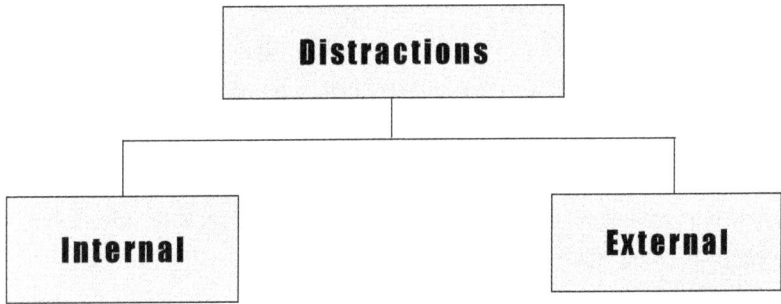

```
                    ┌─────────────────────┐
                    │    Distractions     │
                    └─────────────────────┘
              ┌────────────────┴────────────────┐
      ┌───────────────┐              ┌───────────────┐
      │   Internal    │              │   External    │
      └───────────────┘              └───────────────┘
```

Distractions are derived from one of two source: Internal and External.

Philosophical Resolution

"On the occasion of every act ask thyself: How is this with respect to me? Shall I repent of it? A little time and I am dead, and all is gone. What more do I seek, if what I am now doing is the work of an intelligent living being, and a social being, and one who is under the same law with God?"

- Marcus Aurelius

Mental toughness requires you to address difficult and often controversial questions concerning the use of violence. Philosophical resolution of important martial issues contributes to a warrior's mental confidence and clarity. It is alarming to think of the many years spent by so many warriors achieving the capability to harm others, and even destroy life, with little or no time devoted to the intellectual resolution of questions concerning the ultimate use of violence.

Why are you reading this book? What is your greatest fear? What is the source of your spiritual strength, if any? What is the mind, and what does it mean to be conscious? What is the link between mental power and physical activity? Who are you? How do you know right from wrong?

These are only a few vital questions you must resolve honestly and fully before you can advance to the highest levels of combat awareness. If you haven't begun the quest to formulate the important questions and find your answers, then take a break. It's time to figure out just why you want to know the laws and skills of combat.

A Mixed-Up Moral Conscience

Military, law enforcement, security and self-defense practitioners must take the necessary time to resolve moral issues concerning the use of deadly force in combat. Your religious, philosophical or spiritual beliefs must permit you to justifiably take the life of another in battle. As a result, the warrior is free of apprehension and capable of unleashing violence.

Ironically, one of the biggest obstacles in a combat is often a mixed-up moral conscience. For some people, being forced to use deadly force can create apprehension during a life-and-death encounter. This is often because of incorrect perceptions or misinterpretation of many religious or associated beliefs.

Our culture and system of government are both based on the Judeo-Christian ethic. With this in mind, our parents, teachers, and mentors have ingrained morality issues in us. Therefore, such common statements as "pick on someone your own size" or "don't hit a woman" often leave you with the fatal perception that a smaller or female adversary should be treated differently, when, in reality, anyone - regardless of size, age, gender, race, or appearance - has the potential to destroy you. The Bible can also be easily misinterpreted regarding the use of deadly force. This misinterpretation can be identified in two situations.

Hesitation or The Failure to Act

The commandment "Thou shalt not kill" can cause people to hesitate to employ lethal techniques. A more accurate translation of this commandment is "Thou shalt not murder" (Exodus 20:13) (murder being the unjustifiable taking of another human life). Some people feel they have no right to kill another human being. When using deadly force, your objective is not to take life from another human being, but to stop your enemy from causing you grievous bodily harm or possible death. However, the possibility of the enemy dying should be of no consequence to you. The bottom line is when warranted and justified, killing another person is permitted even under God's law.

Guilt

People who justifiably employ deadly force later suffer some degree of guilt over their actions. They often question their right to take another life in defense of their own. They believe that life is sacred and that only God has the right to take it away. However, in the Bible, if someone tries to kill another unjustifiably, he forfeits the sanctity of his life, and he suffers any consequences brought on by his own actions (Exodus 21:12 and 14). God commands us to protect our lives from others that would take it away unjustifiably. At the same time, God removes the sanctity of a person who chooses to attempt to take the life of someone else unjustifiably.

Responsibility

"If you could kick the person in the pants responsible for most of your trouble, you wouldn't sit for a month."

- Theodore Roosevelt

Responsibility is another core component of mental toughness. Essentially, it means being morally accountable for your own behavior. For example, athletes are responsible for their training and game performance as well as their relentless drive to improve themselves. They must consistently evaluate their performance and determine what must be done to eliminate mistakes in order to achieve peak performance. Consequently, they must take full responsibility for each and every decision and action they make during competition. They must take credit and responsibility for both victories and losses alike.

However, warriors and athletes are only responsible for what they control. Unnecessarily blaming yourself for things that are clearly out of your control is fruitless, and in many cases, self-destructive. The truth is you can still lose a game or battle, despite your best efforts.

The Pitfall of Excuses

Likewise, you must also avoid making excuses for performance failures that are clearly your responsibility. The bottom line is, you and only you must take responsibility for your mistakes and faults. If you make a mistake, own it and learn from it.

Excuses are false reasons or inaccurate justifications used to absolve you of responsibility. However, the truth is they are nothing more than unproductive lies designed to protect your ego. They are inherently dangerous to both the athlete and warrior because they distort reality and prevent the practitioner from learning from his or her mistake. Excuses contradict and undermine the self-awareness required to achieve all forms of peak performance. Therefore, it's in your best interest to consider adopting a zero tolerance policy for excuses.

The Athlete's Responsibility

Regardless of the sport or activity, athletes have a broad range of responsibilities. Some include the following:

- Training (i.e., skill development, conditioning, nutrition and supplementation, proper sleep, etc).
- Attitudes toward the game.
- Attitudes towards teammates, coaches and spectators.
- Attitudes towards the opponent(s).
- Physical actions made during competition.
- Decisions made during competition.
- Arousal control during competition.
- Situational awareness during competition.
- Self-awareness before, during, and after competition.
- Evaluations or appraisals made after your   performance.
- Conduct and behavior off the playing field (i.e., acting as a positive role model for others to emulate).

A Soldier's Responsibility

A professional soldier is responsible for a wide range of individual duties and tasks. However, his most important responsibility is to his platoon. Early on, soldiers are taught essential team building skills that instill the critical importance of watching each other's back. While motion pictures portray Rambo surviving insurmountable odds on his own, the fact is a soldier will always be stronger and stand a greater chance of survival if he is part of a mutually supportive team. In short, team responsibility improves morale, group confidence, and overall military performance.

King Leonidas and his 300 Spartans

A good example of team responsibility can be found in the ancient Greek military formation known as the Phalanx. Perhaps you've seen it demonstrated in the action movie 300, where King Leonidas of Sparta and his 300 Spartans fought against thousands of Persians at the Battle of Thermopylae. Essentially, the phalanx was a cohesive rectangular military formation, consisting of heavy infantry armed with pikes, spears, shields, and similar weapons.

Foot soldiers (called hoplites) were organized into rows, typically about eight ranks deep, and stretching as far as a quarter mile long. Each hoplite carried a large round shield called a hoplon which protected his left side, as well as the man standing to his left. Hoplites would lock their shields together and form a massive wall of spears projecting toward the enemy. The phalanx would then slowly advance to ensure that it would not disturb its formation.

The military strategy of the phalanx formation was if individual foot soldiers stayed in tight formation and acted as a unified group, they could dominate their enemy. It was a team effort that required each foot soldier to trust his life to the man standing next to him. As a military formation, the phalanx was practically unstoppable. It functioned as a slow moving battering ram, designed for direct, bloody combat.

So what does an ancient Greek military formation have to do with teamwork? Actually, a lot! For the phalanx to be successful, it required each Greek hoplite to stand side-by-side with the next foot soldier, to create a densely packed formation. Each man had to trust his life to the man standing next to him. It was this team responsibility that ensured the success of the phalanx and the ultimate survival of the soldiers.

Courage

"Courage, above all things, is the first quality of a warrior."

-Carl von Clausewitz

Courage is at the essential core of any hero. Courage both inspires and validates the warrior. In all times and in all places, courage has been admired and revered, and has become the reason and the rationale for a society's success. But precisely what is courage? In many ways, it is easier to say what courage is not. Courage is not recklessness or foolish risk-taking, nor is it haphazard rage and fury. Instead, courage breeds confidence, resolution, and bravery. As many a fighter will tell you, fear can be intimately entwined with courage. Fear is the stimulus that, biologically speaking, triggers the fight-or-flight response; yet courage is choosing to stay and fight rather than to run away.

Courage Requires Fear

Courage is not the absence of fear, rather it's the ability to perform difficult actions or tasks when you are frightened. It requires you to confront a host of negative emotions and sensations including fear, anxiety, pain, intimidation, and trepidation. As you can imagine, courage is an essential quality for both warriors and athletes.

However, acts of courage are not just limited to elite soldiers or world-class athletes. In fact, everyday living requires courage. Often courage is demonstrated by ordinary people from all walks of life. Take, for example, something as seemingly trivial as a small and insecure teenager confronting an intimidating bully at school or an awkward and unpopular boy asking a girl out on a date. Although small by comparison with major acts of heroism, these trivial actions can be extremely stressful because they require taking action in the face of fear, apprehension, and insecurity. Most importantly, these small acts of courage are critical because they serve as steppingstones to greater acts of courage in the future.

The Coward and the Hero

Both heroes and cowards alike experience fear. However, the difference between the two is how each one handles it. When a coward experiences fear he will either freeze in his tracks or try to escape from the threat or danger. Conversely, when a hero experiences fear, he confronts it head-on by taking positive actions to overcome the obstacle or challenge.

What is Fear?

Understanding fear and it's effects on your mind and body is the first step to managing it. Essentially, fear is a strong and unpleasant emotional reaction to a real or perceived threat. If uncontrolled, fear leads to panic. Then it's too late to adequately perform.

The Three Levels of Fear

To prevent the negative effects of fear, you need to understand its levels and dynamics. For analysis, I have categorized fear into three different levels, listed in order of intensity:

1. **Fright** - quick or sudden fear.

2. **Panic**- overpowering fear.

3. **Terror** - crippling or immobilizing fear.

While these three levels of fear vary in degrees of stress, they all have one common root response: the fight-or-flight response.

What is The Fight-or-Flight Response?

Whenever a person, or any animal for that matter, feels threatened or frightened, certain physiological changes occur. They start in the brain when the hypothalamus sends strong impulses to the pituitary gland, causing it to release a hormone (ACTH) that stimulates the adrenal glands to release other hormones into the bloodstream.

Ultimately every nerve and muscle is involved. This adrenaline will cause an increased heart rate with a corresponding increase in respiration and blood pressure. Your muscles will tense up, you will start to sweat, and your mouth will go dry. In addition, your digestive system will shut down to allow a better supply of blood to the muscles. Your hair will stand on end (piloerection). Your pupils will enlarge so that your vision can improve. Your hand and limbs will also begin to tremble. Once these biochemical mechanisms and processes are fully engaged - and it takes only nanoseconds - your body will be in the fight-or-flight mode.

Arousal Control

For most people, the fight-or-flight response has a debilitating effect. They panic or freeze up, and fear then becomes a powerful weapon of the opponent. Therefore, it is critically important that you learn to control the physiological and psychological response to make it work for you and not against you in a critical situation. This is referred to as "arousal control."

The first step to controlling arousal is to accept the fact that the fight-or-flight response is a natural human response. In fact, it's one of Mother Nature's best ways of helping you survive a stressful situation. You've got to take advantage of this assistance by using the energy of the adrenaline surge to augment your physical performance.

Second, harness the fight-or-flight response by preparing yourself thoroughly for the danger that may one day confront you. Developing the psychological and physical skills of your craft will lead to a personal self-confidence. In turn, this confidence leads to an inner calm. Inner calm is the environment necessary for peak performance.

Third, actively employ coping techniques like meditation, mental visualization, positive self-talk, and controlled breathing skills to manage the immediate effects of stress, anxiety, and fear (much more will be discussed in chapter 6).

Fourth, develop a keen sense of self-awareness. Never stop assessing your state of mind and reactions to different stressful situations. For example, the next time you are startled by something, pay close attention. What was it that startled you and why? Did you freeze up? What did you see? What did you hear? Were you trembling and breathing heavily? Was your mind clear or distracted? Exactly what were you thinking about? How much detail can you remember? Did you make any tactical errors in your responses? These are only a few of the questions you should answer over and over again as you go

The 10 Best Mental Toughness Exercises

through the process of preparing yourself psychologically.

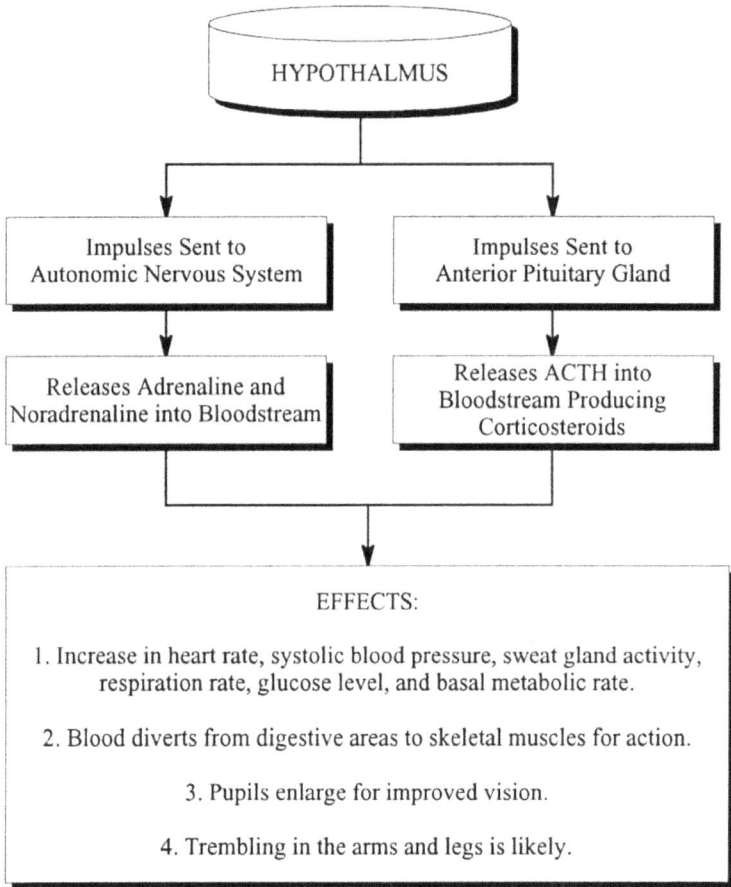

```
                    ┌──────────────────────┐
                    │     HYPOTHALMUS      │
                    └──────────────────────┘
```

Impulses Sent to Autonomic Nervous System	Impulses Sent to Anterior Pituitary Gland
Releases Adrenaline and Noradrenaline into Bloodstream	Releases ACTH into Bloodstream Producing Corticosteroids

EFFECTS:

1. Increase in heart rate, systolic blood pressure, sweat gland activity, respiration rate, glucose level, and basal metabolic rate.

2. Blood diverts from digestive areas to skeletal muscles for action.

3. Pupils enlarge for improved vision.

4. Trembling in the arms and legs is likely.

Another method of psychological preparation is written analysis. For example, write down five different hypothetical scenarios that truly frighten you. These scenarios could take place anywhere. Be specific with your details. Make certain to include the following relevant factors:

1. The source of danger and threat.

2. The time of day.

3. The environment.

4. Your mental, physical and emotional state during the crisis.

4. Any other relevant factors to your scenario.

Once you've completed these scenarios, have your coach or instructor identify the specific factors that elicit reasonable fear and then adjust your training to meet your concerns.

Possible Physiological Responses To Fear

1. Enlarged pupils

2. Dry mouth

3. Trembling hands

4. Cold, clammy hands

5. Increased heart rate

6. Shutdown of digestive system

7. Tense muscles

8. Sudden adrenaline surge

9. Hair stands on end

10. Enhanced alertness

How to Develop Courage

Courage is a tool that enables you to confront the fear. Like any tool, it can be developed and sharpened, so you'll be adequately prepared to deal with life's obstacles. When properly developed, courage gives you strength and empowerment to achieve your goal. It affords you the mental composure to perform risky and perhaps dangerous tasks with dignity and grace. Developing courage is a process that takes time. The goal is to take small steps that will progressively lead to significant acts of courage. What follows are a few guidelines to help you develop courage.

The 10 Best Mental Toughness Exercises

1.   First, understand that courage is not the absence of fear. It is action made in the face of fear.

2.   Realize that courage is critical to your survival. Intellectualize the alternative - living a fearful life!

3.   Make it a habit to listen to or read the daily news. Pay attention to all stories relating to acts of bravery and heroism.

4.   If you ever have the opportunity, talk to military veterans, law enforcement officers, firefighters, and other types of emergency responders. Their real-life stories are truly inspiring and often filled with acts of courage.

5.   Get into the habit of stepping out of your personal comfort zone. Do things that you wouldn't normally do. For example, if you are a shy person, make a daily goal to initiate a friendly conversation with a stranger. Or ask someone out on a date. Remember, the goal is to take baby steps that will progressively build up your courage.

6.   If you are someone who plays role-playing video games, consider only playing "permanent death" or dead-is-dead versions of the game. While this might seem trivial to non-gamers, the consequences are huge for people who invest hundreds of hours of their lives playing a game. Playing dead-is-dead, compared to just reloading a saved game, brings an entirely new dimension to gaming. Every action has tremendous repercussions for the player. It's not unusual for many gamers who play dead-is-dead to experience intense emotions such as stress, anxiety, apprehension, and even trepidation.

7.   Learn how to mask your fear. Masking is the process of "staying cool" and concealing your emotions from your opponent when you are experiencing fear or trepidation.

It is the process of manipulating and managing your body language (both facial expressions and body gestures). In many cases, displaying signs of fear, anger, trepidation or weariness will just fuel your opponent's fire. Unfortunately, masking cannot hide some involuntary physical reactions (i.e., excessive perspiring, heavy breathing, trembling hands, etc.). However, the good news is you can cover them up by quickly moving about, diverting the opponent's attention elsewhere, etc.

8. Regularly use coping techniques like meditation, mental visualization, positive self-talk, and controlled breathing skills to manage your fears.

9. Depending on your situation, you can use scenario-based training and other stress inoculation techniques to manage fear.

10. Strive to master the knowledge, skills and attitudes of your craft.

11. Understand and accept the physiological responses to the fight-or-flight response.

12. Evaluate your past responses to crisis situations. What did you do right? What did you do wrong?

The 10 Best Mental Toughness Exercises

Chapter Three

The 10 Best Mental Toughness Exercises

Cognitive Training for Mental Toughness

In this chapter, I will be teaching you several cognitive exercises to develop and improve your level of mental toughness. Some of these exercises can also be used as coping tools during the immediate stress and anxiety of a high-performance situation. Let's start with creative visualization.

Mental Visualization

Through years of research and training, I found mental visualization to be a fascinating subject. Briefly stated, visualization is the formation of mental images to bring about desired goals ranging anywhere from improved lifestyles and health to better job performance and athletic ability. Established research indicates that mental images cause brain activity identical to that produced by an actual experience. Even if the image is unrealistic or logically impossible, the body will still produce a response that stimulates every cell in the body. There is no doubt that visualization can significantly improve mental toughness. To truly reap the benefits, however, you must make certain that your images are clear and strong. In essence, you must feel, taste, smell, and here the visualized scenario.

Visualization for Mental Toughness

Visualization serves many purposes in mental toughness training. As a training aid, visualization improves concentration, selective attention, self-confidence, instrumental aggression and helps maintain motivation during grueling workouts.

In sports, practice and training will only take you so far. In order to maximize your athletic potential, you must learn to use the mind's eye to further enhance your skills and abilities. The same applies to combat performance during extremely dangerous and hostile encounters. For example, visualizing strategic solutions to various high-risk combat scenarios also enhances performance and reduces the possibility of making tactical mistakes.

How to do it

Visualization is a natural and relatively simple exercise. The good news is the more often you use it, the easier it becomes. Effective visualization requires a quiet place, free from distractions, for at least 20 minutes. Turn off your cell phone and tell your partner or roommates that you do not wish to be disturbed. It is vital that you have peace and quiet.

Every visualization session must be undertaken in a relaxed state, the preparatory state for visualization. To attain a state of relaxation, you must first sit in a chair or lie on a couch or bed. If sitting, make certain your back is straight, your arms are uncrossed, and your feet are both on the floor. If lying down, place your arms at your side. You may want to put a pillow under your head.

There are various relaxation exercises you can perform. One of the easiest to learn is the tensing – releasing method. To begin, close your eyes and begin to breathe slowly and deeply for approximately 2 minutes. The next step requires you to tense every muscle in your body all at once. Clench your fists and your feet. Tighten your jaw and facial muscles. Tense your shoulders, chest, back, legs, and buttocks. Hold the tension for approximately 10 seconds then in one concentrated effort, let go and allow the tension to flow out of your body.

Visualization Examples

In this section, I am going to show you how to use visualization techniques to improve specific aspects of mental toughness. Here are two examples of what you can do with mental imagery. Let's begin with improving your training performance.

Training Performance Visualization

Before visualizing your training event, you must first have a clear mental picture of yourself. Begin by closing your eyes and visualizing yourself in a relaxed and peaceful state. Visualize your physical characteristics. Imagine your face. Note your eyes, nose, mouth, and chin. Observe the length and color of your hair. Now, look at your torso and concentrate on your chest and shoulders. See the veins that run up and down your biceps, forearms, and hands. Focus on your quadriceps, hamstrings, calves, and feet. Concentrate on the clarity of the vision. It may be helpful to glance at a picture of yourself occasionally to get a clear image.

Now, visualize yourself in a very serious training environment, maybe at a nearby gym. Visualize your surroundings. For example, envision a large, dingy and well-equipped gym. Feel the dank air against your face, neck and arms. Smell the subtle odor of sweat as you walk past three athletes working out. Listen to the sound of iron plates crashing to the floor. Remember, mental imagery is not limited to the visual. Concentrate on crystallizing this entire scenario. This may require you to run it numerous times in your head to bring it into full focus.

Next, picture yourself performing various weight training exercises. For example, you are now going to perform heavy squats. Envision yourself confidently walk up to the squat rack and load six 45-pound plates on the Olympic bar. See yourself tighten a weight lifting belt around your waist as you approach the bar. Imagine resting the back of your shoulders under the bar while holding it in place with both of your hands. Picture a solid stance with your feet approximately shoulder width apart from each other. Feel the heaviness of the weight and the strain in your muscles as you lift the heavy bar from the rack. Now, visualize the perfect execution of a leg squat - head up, back straight, and your feet flush against the floor. Watch yourself breathe deeply as you slowly lower your body to the squat position. Imagine yourself exploding upward back to the starting position. Experience the sensation of pure confidence as you start another repetition. Continue this mental imagery for each and every repetition in your set.

Now, visualize how you feel after your leg workout. Imagine the distinct soreness in your leg muscles. Feel them cramp and ache from complete exhaustion. Picture how difficult it is to walk up a flight of stairs after training your legs. Experience that priceless feeling of accomplishment and achievement as you amble your way to your car.

Instrumental Aggression Visualization

This visualization scenario is going to focus on developing instrumental aggression for combat performance. Start by visualizing yourself in a dangerous environmental setting, maybe walking through an alley in some seedy part of town. Feel the cool night air rush your body. Envision the gloomy brick buildings that surround you. Smell the rotten garbage as you walk past the overloaded trash cans. Listen to the sound of cars driving in the distance, hear an alley cat cry from hunger.

Now, imagine a distant figure lurking in the shadows, slowly approaching you. Mentally conjure up a person, giving him strong physical characteristics. Make him dangerous and threatening – perhaps a tall and powerful mesomorph. Begin with his facial characteristics and visualize his entire body. Smell the repulsive stench that radiates from his unbathed body. Give this imaginary assailant a criminal motive and a voice to express it. Feel your heart accelerate and your adrenaline soar. Don't forget to visualize essential tactical factors, such as the opponent's range, positioning, weapon capability, and state of mind. Again, it might be necessary to run the scenario several times in your mind to crystallize the confrontation.

Next, visualize an extreme reversal in your mentality – the aggressive side of your temperament. Watch yourself transform into a calm and controlled warrior. You are dangerous, courageous, and free from distractions. Your mind is razor sharp and focused on the confrontation.

Visualize your chest cavity expand as oxygen fills your lungs. Hose like veins protrude from your temple, and your face begins to grin with anticipation. You are ready to fight! You assume a fighting stance, and the storm of destruction begins. See yourself move forward with a brutal and vicious compound attack. The fighting techniques you choose are entirely up to you; however, be certain that they accurately relate to the circumstance, environment, range, and targets presented by the imaginary assailant. During your attack, picture the opponents bone shatter as you deliver powerful blows. Listen to him groan in pain and whimper in agony. Finally, watch the adversary fall to the ground, incapacitated and harmless.

Try visualizing the scenario at different mental speeds. Experiment with different combative scenarios. Change the environment, circumstance, opponent, range, and level of use-of-force. Be creative; remember, no two self-defense altercations are going to be the same.

Meditation and Mental Toughness

Meditation is a technique whereby the practitioner achieves a state of deep physiological and mental repose. It has been used throughout the centuries by the Indian yogis, Taoists, Buddhists, and the mystics to achieve self-enlightenment. It wasn't until the 60s that Westerners recognize the value of meditation for reducing stress, muscle tension, pulse rate, high blood pressure, and other ailments.

Meditation serves several purposes in mental toughness training. It develops both self-discipline and self-awareness. Meditation also enhances concentration. Through its practice, you learn to eliminate both internal and external distractions from your mind. Believe it or not, meditation also cultivates characteristics of instrumental aggression. Through consistent practice, you can acquire an emotionless state of mind that is essential for high-risk combat operations. Meditation can also be used to clear the warrior's mind after a dangerous and stressful combat event. Stress and anxiety are replaced with inner peace, patience and a state of well-being.

How to do it

Effective meditation requires a quiet environment and freedom from distractions for at least 30 minutes. A quiet and comfortable room will suffice. There is no need to burn incense or decorate your room in an oriental motif. Just keep it plain and simple. Meditation can also be practiced outdoors, as long as the location is quiet and peaceful.

Posture is another important factor. You want to be as comfortable as possible when meditating. There are many different types of meditative postures. The most common is the seated, cross-legged position, where the legs are crossed with the feet under the thighs. The head is balanced and facing forward, the torso is erect, and the hands are placed on the knees. This is by far the most comfortable and unrestricted posture. I do not recommend lying down; you should not be so relaxed that the mind becomes unfocused.

Once you are in a comfortable position, close your eyes and begin to breathe slowly and deeply, in through your nose and out through your mouth. The goal is to relax. The next step is the most difficult. You want to eliminate any thoughts from your mind. The objective is to remain mentally void. Don't let your mind wander or visualize. You want to reach a state of "nothingness." If thoughts or images do enter your mind, don't concentrate on them. Just allow them to drift from your consciousness. Concentrating on "nothing" can be difficult and very frustrating. It becomes easier with constant practice, however. If your schedule permits, meditate every day. If your time is limited, three times a week will suffice. Make sure each session lasts at least 20 minutes.

Remember that results will not come overnight. Like any worthwhile endeavor, meditation requires practice and time.

Controlled Breathing

Controlled breathing is a very useful technique for managing the stress and anxiety associated with a variety of high-performance tasks. This form of tactical breathing can be used by warriors and athletes. However, it's especially helpful for arousal control during high-risk duties such as those found in military, law enforcement, and private security work.

All of us, at one time or another, have experienced the uncontrolled breathing pattern associated with fear or extreme stress. If you recall, it was loud, fast and shallow. Therefore, the objective of controlled breathing is to do the exact opposite. By employing slow and controlled breathing, you will be able to regain control of your emotional state. Deep and steady breathing quickly shifts your mind and body into a more relaxed state, so you can efficiently perform your task or mission during a crisis situation.

How to do it

Initially, controlled breathing should be practiced in a quiet place, free from distractions, for at least 15 minutes. It's best to practice while sitting in a chair or lying on a comfortable couch or bed. If sitting, make certain your back is straight, your arms are uncrossed, and your feet are both on the floor. If lying down, place your arms at your side. You may want to put a pillow under your head.

Next, close your eyes and relax your body. Begin by inhaling deeply and steadily for 4 seconds. Let your lungs fill and expand with air. Hold this for one second and then exhale steadily for 4 seconds. Allow all of the air to expel from your mouth. Repeat this process for a minimum of 15 minutes. Advanced practitioners can also incorporate controlled breathing exercises with mental visualization scenarios. The more you practice controlled breathing, the faster you'll be able to bring about its relaxation response.

Once you master the basics, you can practice controlled breathing during idle times. For example, when you are waiting in a long line or when you are stuck in a traffic jam. However, controlled breathing is best used before, during and after a high-pressure performance situation.

Positive Thinking & Self-Talk

Many people underestimate the power of positive thinking. As a matter of fact, research suggests numerous health benefits from positive and optimistic thinking. Some include:

- Increased longevity
- Greater resistance to illness
- Improved productivity
- Improved self-esteem
- Improved physical well-being
- Reduced risk of heart disease
- Greater coping skills during stressful events

Positive thinking is especially important for mental toughness.

The 10 Best Mental Toughness Exercises

In order to effectively overcome adversity, you must possess the self-confidence and personal belief that you can overcome any obstacle or hardship. However, don't confuse positive thinking with arrogance, self-delusion or blind hope. Positive thinking must be predicated on competency. You must, in fact, possess the actual skills and attributes necessary to address your adverse situation.

Positive Self-Talk

Positive thinking is the environment necessary for effective self-talk. Self-talk is the internal dialogue you have with yourself during a stressful performance situation, and it's based on your beliefs, assumptions, and individual perceptions. This internal dialogue is essential to identifying and solving problems during a performance event. In fact, positive self-talk during performance situations improves attention control and will help eliminate self-doubts and false assumptions, which can destroy peak performance.

Positive self-talk is a skill, and like any skill, it takes practice. Here are several techniques that will get you started in the right direction.

- Be self-aware and learn to catch yourself when you are thinking negatively.

- Whenever a negative self-statement is made, quickly replace it with a positive and optimistic one. For example, change "I suck!" to "I love this challenge."

- Interrupt negative self-talk with a positive visual image of yourself (i.e., completing the mission, scoring a touchdown, defeating the enemy, etc.).

- Regularly visualize yourself in positive and favorable situations.

- Intentionally use positive words in your inner dialogues, or when talking with other people.

- Approach every situation or circumstance with favorable expectations.
- Make it a habit to take control of stressful situations.
- Try to associate with people who are positive and upbeat.

Using Cue Words

A cue word is a unique word or personal statement that helps focus your attention on the execution of a skill, instead of its outcome. It is also a very effective thought-stopping technique for halting unwanted thoughts during a crisis. For example, since the brain can only focus on one thing at a time, concentrating on a specific cue word is a very effective way of taking your mind off negative thoughts during a performance event. Cue words, however, should be positive, personal and short. They can also include action statements or instructional phrases.

Sample Cue Words or Statements:

- *"Attack!"*
- *"Explode!"*
- *"Tough!"*
- *"Dominate!"*
- *"Shoot!"*
- *"Fight"*
- *"Focus!"*
- *"Relax!"*
- *"Hit!"*
- *"Punch!"*
- *"Move!"*
- *"Steady!"*

The 10 Best Mental Toughness Exercises

- *"Power!"*
- *"Hold on!"*
- *"Swing!"*
- *"Jump!"*
- *"Faster!"*
- *"In Control!"*
- *"Ready, Set, Go!"*
- *"Eye on the Ball!"*
- *"Crush him!"*

Optical Illusion Exercises

The following exercises are designed to improve your selective attention and concentration skills. Each drawing is an optical illusion that presents one of two different perceptual images. The goal is to concentrate and focus exclusively on only one perceptual image for a specified period of time. Start off with 15 seconds and progressively work your way up to 5 minutes. Remember, if your attention breaks (and you see the other image), you must start over again. This may sound easy to some, but I assure you that it is not.

1. Beginner level - 15 seconds.

2. Intermediate level - 30 seconds.

3. Skilled level - 90 seconds.

4. Advanced level - 3 minutes.

5. Mental Mastery level - 5 minutes.

The Rubin Vase

What do you see? Is it a curved vase or two faces looking directly at each other? Concentrate and focus on only one perceptual image.

Young Lady or Old Woman

What do you see? Is it a young lady or old woman? Concentrate and focus on only one perceptual image.

The 10 Best Mental Toughness Exercises

The Face

What do you see? Is it a woman standing next to a tree or a face staring at you? Concentrate and focus on only one perceptual image.

Woman Reading a Book or Old Man

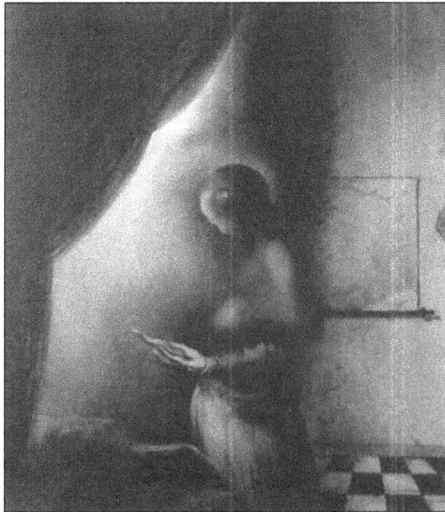

What do you see? Is it a woman reading a book or the face of an old man? Concentrate and focus on only one perceptual image.

The Devil Face

What do you see? Is it a devil face or a group of women standing in front of their own reflections in a mirror? Concentrate and focus on only one perceptual image.

Bifurcation Training

Bifurcation training is ideal for improving selective attention and mental concentration. This exercise requires the practitioner to perform a particular physical performance action while simultaneously executing an unrelated mental task. The physical performance could be anything that involves technical skill and movement (i.e., a golf swing, tennis serve, baseball pitch, football forward pass, arrest and control maneuver, target practice, punching combination, etc). The mental task portion of the drill, however, requires you either to solve a mathematical equation or recite a verse or nursery rhyme.

The 10 Best Mental Toughness Exercises

The following bifurcation drills will use a striking combination or "compound attack" as the physical performance action. Let's begin with the pledge drill.

Pledge Drill

This exercise requires that you verbally recite the pledge of allegiance. While you are reciting the pledge your training partner yells, "Go!" and you are to immediately launch a preselected compound attack in the air. The key is to deliver a flurry of full-speed, full-force strikes while continuing to recite the pledge in a calm and controlled manner. It's critical that you do not alter the tone, pitch, volume, or tempo of your voice when delivering your assault.

Nursery Rhyme Drill (beginner level)

This exercise is similar to "the pledge" except that it requires you to verbally recite a simple children's nursery rhyme, such as "Mary Had a Little Lamb" or "Hickory, Dickory, Dock." Once again, while you are reciting the rhyme, your training partner yells, "Go!" and you are to immediately launch a preselected compound attack in the air without disturbing the vocalization of the rhyme. Once again, it's critical not to alter the tonality of your voice when delivering your assault.

Tongue Twister (intermediate level)

The tongue twister is an intermediate-level drill that requires you to slowly and repeatedly recite a tongue twister, such as "She sells seashells on the seashore of Seychelles" or "Peter Piper picked a peck of pickled peppers." While you are reciting this statement, your training partner yells, "Go!" and you must immediately launch a preselected compound attack in the air. Once again, it's critical that you do not disturb the vocalization or alter the tone, pitch, volume, or tempo of your voice when delivering your assault.

The Alphabet Drill (advanced level)

The "alphabet" is a more advanced drill. Your objective here is to slowly recite the alphabet backward. At some point during your recitation, your training partner is to yell, "Go!" and you are to immediately launch a preselected compound attack in the air while continuing to recite the alphabet backward. Don't get frustrated with this exercise; it's designed to challenge you.

Sample Compound Attacks

What follows are five compound attacks that can be employed when conducting bifurcation training. A "compound attack" is the logical sequence of two or more techniques thrown in strategic succession. For example, a lead straight punch followed immediately by a rear cross is considered to be a compound attack. There are infinite fighting combinations you can perform during bifurcation training. *(For more information about specific fighting techniques, please see the appendix of this book.)*

When executing your compound attack, make certain your strikes are delivered with speed, power, and proper form. You can also perform these combinations in front of a mirror, on the heavy bag or the focus mitts.

1. **Lead straight/rear cross/lead straight**
2. **Push kick/rear uppercut/lead uppercut/rear hook punch**
3. **Lead straight/rear cross/lead hook punch/rear hook punch**
4. **Hook kick/rear hook punch/lead hook punch/rear uppercut**
5. **Rear hook punch/lead uppercut/rear uppercut/lead hook punch**

Opportunity Training

Opportunity training is used during idle times or when a unique situation presents the "opportunity" to practice your mental toughness skills. Here are a few examples:

Insomnia

All of us suffer from insomnia. Insomnia is generally caused by stress and anxiety from a variety of issues and factors, some include relationship and financial problems, job loss, moving, divorce, illness, emotional or physical discomfort, and environmental factors like noise, light, or extreme temperatures.

If you can't sleep, use it as an opportunity to work on your attention control skills. Practice controlled breathing and focus on blocking out the negative and stressful thoughts that are keeping you up. Continue doing this until you fall back asleep.

Delayed Trip

Imagine being stuck on an airplane for 6 hours on the runway. It sounds like hell, and it is. Use this situation as an opportunity to practice your mental visualization skills. For example, close your eyes and begin visualizing positive and vivid images, such as the plane taking off, the view from the window, the plane landing, and the feelings you will experience when you reach your destination. Keep visualizing these images until your plane actually takes off.

Crying Baby

Nothing claws at your brain more than a baby screaming on the top of his lungs. Instead of leaving the area, use this as an opportunity to develop your attention control skills. Try to filter out and ignore the high-pitch crying and blood-curdling screams. Direct your attention to something else in your immediate environment. For example, try memorizing lines of a verse during the tantrum. The turmoil around you can work to strengthen both your selective attention and concentration.

Tattoos

Getting tattooed is no picnic. As a matter of fact, it can be downright miserable. Especially, if you are having a lot of work done on a sensitive part of your body, such as the wrist, elbow or ribs.

Initially, getting tattooed might seem exciting, but I can assure you the excitement wears off real fast. The process of being tattooed is painful, boring and mentally draining. A few hours "in the chair" will make you want to scream and rip your hair out.

However, if you must get tattooed, use it as an opportunity to develop your mental resilience and attention control skills. Try to disassociate your mind from the constant pain and irritation of the needle digging relentlessly into your skin. Focus and direct your attention to something else in the room, perhaps a picture on the wall or an object on a table in front of you. Try to maintain this form of attention control for the duration of your tattoo session.

Reading and Research

The intellectual, or academic, aspects of mental toughness training cannot be overstated. You must possess an insatiable desire to learn and grow to your full potential. Academic research involves voracious reading. The body of printed materials on mental toughness has grown astronomically.

Try to read anything you can get your hands on. However, don't make the common mistake of passively reading material. Get into the habit of dissecting and noting literature. Strategically sound theories and unique training concepts should be noted and remembered. Books should be read over and over again until practical ideas are intellectually solidified. Finally, always read material with an open mind balanced with healthy skepticism.

Appendix

Combat Skills

In this section, I am going to teach you the foundational combat skills required to perform some of the mental toughness drills featured in this book. These basic skills include the fighting stance, mobility and footwork, punching, kicking, blocking, and parrying techniques. Let's begin with the fighting stance.

The Fighting Stance

The fighting stance defines your ability to execute both offensive and defensive techniques, and it will play a material role in the outcome of a combat situation. It stresses strategic soundness and simplicity over complexity and style. The fighting stance also facilitates optimum execution of your body weapons while simultaneously protecting your vital targets against quick counter strikes.

The fighting stance is designed around the centerline. The centerline is an imaginary vertical line running through the center of the body, from the top of your head to the bottom of the groin. Most of your vital targets are situated along this line, including the head, throat, solar plexus, and groin. Obviously, you want to avoid directly exposing your centerline to the assailant. To achieve this, position your feet and body at a 45-degree angle

Pictured here, a right lead fighting stance.

from the opponent. This moves your body targets back and away from direct strikes but leaves you strategically positioned to attack.

When assuming a fighting stance, place your strongest and most coordinated side forward. For example, a right-handed person stands with his or her right side toward the assailant. Keeping your strongest side forward enhances the speed, power, and accuracy of your strike. This doesn't mean that you should never practice fighting from your other side. You must be capable of fighting from both sides, and you should spend equal practice time on the left and right stances.

Many people make the costly mistake of stepping forward to assume a fighting stance. Do not do this! This action only moves you closer to your assailant before your protective structure is soundly established. Moving closer to your assailant also dramatically reduces your defensive reaction time. So get into the habit of stepping backward to assume your stance. Practice this daily until it becomes a natural and economical movement.

How to Assume a Fighting Stance

When assuming your fighting stance, place your feet about shoulder width apart. Keep your knees bent and flexible. Think of your legs as power springs to launch you through the ranges of unarmed combat (kicking, punching, and grappling range).

Mobility is also important, as we'll discuss later. All footwork and strategic movement should be performed on the balls of your feet. Your weight distribution is also an important factor. Since combat is dynamic, your weight distribution will frequently change. However, when stationary, keep 50 percent of your body weight on each leg and always be in control of it.

The hands are aligned one behind the other along your centerline. The lead arm is held high and bent at approximately 90 degrees. The rear arm is kept back by the chin. Arranged this way, the hands not only protect the upper centerline but also allow quick deployment of your body weapons. When holding your guard, do not tighten your shoulder or arm muscles prior to striking. Stay relaxed and loose. Finally, keep your chin slightly angled down. This diminishes target size and reduces the likelihood of a paralyzing blow to your chin or a lethal strike to your throat.

The best method for practicing your fighting stance is in front of a full-length mirror. Place the mirror in an area that allows sufficient room for movement; a garage or basement is perfect. Stand in front of the mirror, far enough away to see your entire body. Stand naturally with your arms relaxed at your sides. Now close your eyes and quickly assume your fighting stance. Open your eyes and check for flaws. Look for low hand guards, improper foot positioning or body angle, rigid shoulders and knees, etc. Drill this way repeatedly, working from both the right and left side. Practice this until your fighting stance becomes second nature.

Footwork & Mobility

Next are footwork and mobility. I define mobility as the ability to move your body quickly and freely, which is accomplished through basic footwork. The safest footwork involves quick, economical steps performed on the balls of your feet, while you remain relaxed and balanced. Keep in mind that balance is your most important consideration.

Basic footwork can be used for both offensive and defensive purposes, and it is structured around four general directions: forward, backward, right, and left. However, always remember this footwork rule of thumb: Always move the foot closest to the direction you want to go first, and let the other foot follow an equal distance. This prevents cross-stepping, which can cost you your life in a high-risk combat situation.

Basic Footwork Movements

1. Moving forward (advance)- from your fighting stance, first move your front foot forward (approximately 12 inches) and then move your rear foot an equal distance.

2. Moving backward (retreat) - from your fighting stance, first move your rear foot backward (approximately 12 inches) and then move your front foot an equal distance.

3. Moving right (sidestep right) - from your fighting stance, first move your right foot to the right (approximately 12 inches) and then move your left foot an equal distance.

4. Moving left (sidestep left) - from your fighting stance, first move your left foot to the left (approximately 12 inches) and then move your right foot an equal distance.

Practice these four movements for 10 to 15 minutes a day in front of a full-length mirror. In a couple weeks, your footwork should be quick, balanced, and natural.

Circling Right and Left

Strategic circling is an advanced form of footwork where you will use your front leg as a pivot point. This type of movement can also be used defensively to evade an overwhelming assault or to strike the opponent from various strategic angles. Strategic circling can be performed from either a left or right stance.

Circling left (from a left stance) - this means you'll be moving your body around the opponent in a clockwise direction. From a left stance, step 8 to 12 inches to the left with your left foot, then use your left leg as a pivot point and wheel your entire rear leg to the left until the correct stance and positioning is acquired.

Circling right (from a right stance) - from a right stance, step 8 to 12 inches to the right with your right foot, then use your right leg as a pivot point and wheel your entire rear leg to the right until the correct stance and positioning is acquired.

Kicking Techniques

While there are a myriad of kicking techniques in the martial arts world, we are only going to focus on five basic skills. They are:

- **Push kick (from the front and back legs)**
- **Side kick (from the front leg)**
- **Hook kick (from the front and back legs)**

Push Kick (front leg)

1. To perform the kick, begin from a fighting stance.
2. While maintaining your balance, shift your weight onto your back leg and raise your front leg up (your front knee should be bent at approximately 90 degrees).
3. Next, thrust with your hips and drive the ball of your front foot into the target.
4. After contact is made with the target, quickly retract your leg to the starting position. Remember to always keep your hands up when performing kicking techniques.

When performing the push kick be certain to make contact with the ball of your foot and not your toes. Striking the opponent with your toes can easily lead to a severe injury.

Push Kick (back leg)

1. To perform the kick, begin from a fighting stance.
2. While maintaining your balance, push your back foot off the ground and shift your weight to your front leg (your rear

knee should be bent at approximately 90 degrees).

3. Next, thrust with your hips and drive the ball of your foot into the target.

4. After contact is made with the target, quickly retract your leg to the starting position. Again, make certain to make contact with the ball of your foot and not your toes.

Pictured here, a push kick delivered from the front leg.

Side Kick (front leg)

1. To perform the kick, begin from a fighting stance.

2. While maintaining your balance, lean back and shift your weight onto your rear leg while simultaneously pivoting your body so your centerline is approximately 90 degrees from the opponent.

3. Raise your front knee up and close to your body (this is called the "chamber" position).

4. Next, use your hips and thrust your front leg forcefully into

the target. Contact is made with the heel of your foot.

5. After contact is made with the target, retract your leg to the starting position.

Pictured here, a side kick.

Hook Kick (front leg)

1. To perform the kick, begin from a fighting stance.

2. While maintaining your balance, lean back slightly and shift your weight to your rear leg.

3. Simultaneously raise your front knee up and towards the opponent.

4. Next, quickly twist your front hip and swing your lead leg forcefully into the opponent. Your front knee should be slightly bent when impact is made with the target. Avoid snapping your knee when performing the kick. Contact should be made with either the dorsum of your foot or shin bone.

5. After contact is made with the opponent, bring your leg back to the starting position.

Hook Kick (back leg)

1. To perform the kick, begin from a fighting stance.

2. While maintaining your balance, push off the back foot and shift your weight forward.

3. Next, raise your rear knee up and twist your hips forward as you swing your rear leg forcefully into the opponent.

4. Your rear knee should be slightly bent when impact is made with the target. Avoid snapping your knee when performing the hook kick. Once again, contact should be made with either the dorsum of your foot or shin bone.

5. After contact is made with the target, bring your leg back to the starting position.

The hook kick.

Punching Techniques

In this section, I'm going to teach you four different punching skills that can be used in some of the mental toughness exercises. They are:

- **Lead straight**
- **Rear cross**
- **Hook punch**
- **Uppercut punch**

The Lead Straight Punch

The lead straight is a linear punch thrown from your lead arm, and contact is made with the center knuckle. To execute the technique, perform the following steps.

1. Start off in a fighting stance with both of your hands held up in the guard position. Your fists should be lightly clenched with both of your elbows pointing to the ground.

2. Simultaneously step toward the opponent and twist your front waist and shoulder forward as you snap your front arm into the target.

3. When delivering the punch, remember not to lock out your arm as this will have a "pushing effect" on the target.

4. Quickly retract your arm back to the starting position.

5. One common mistake when throwing the punch is to let it deflect off to the side of the target. Also, keep in mind that lead straight punches can be delivered to the opponent's head or body. Targets for the lead straight include the opponent's nose, chin, and solar plexus.

Pictured here, a lead straight punch.

Rear Cross

The rear cross is considered the heavy artillery of punches and it's thrown from your rear arm. To execute the punch, perform the following steps:

1. Start off in a fighting stance with both of your hands held up in the guard position. Your fists should be lightly clenched with both of your elbows pointing to the ground.

2. Next, quickly twist your rear hips and shoulders forward as you snap your rear arm into the target. Proper waist twisting and weight transfer is of paramount importance to the rear cross. You must shift your weight from your rear foot to your lead leg as you throw the punch.

3. To maximize the impact of the punch, make certain that your fist is positioned horizontally. Avoid overextending the blow or exposing your chin during its execution.

4. Once again, do not lock out your arm when throwing the

punch. Let the power of the blow sink into the target before you retract it back to the starting position.

The rear cross.

Hook Punch

The hook is another devastating punch in your arsenal, yet it's also one of the most difficult to master. This punch can be performed from either your front or rear hand, and it can be delivered to both high or low targets.

1. Start in a fighting stance with your hand guard held up. Both of your elbows should be pointing to the ground, and your fists clenched loosely.

2. Next, quickly and smoothly, raise your elbow up so that your arm is parallel to the ground while simultaneously torquing your shoulder, hip, and foot into the direction of the blow.

3. When delivering the strike, be certain your arm is bent at least ninety degrees and that your wrist and forearm are kept

straight throughout the movement.

4. As you throw the punch, your fist is positioned vertically. The elbow should be locked when contact is made with the target. Remember to simultaneously tighten your fists when impact is made with the target. This action will allow your punch to travel with optimum speed and efficiency, and it will also augment the impact power of your strike.

5. Return to the starting position.

The lead hook punch.

Uppercut Punch

The uppercut is a another powerful punch that can be delivered from both the lead and rear arm. To execute the blow, perform the following steps.

1. Start off in a fighting stance with both of your hands held up in the guard position. Your fists should be lightly clenched with both of your elbows pointing to the ground.

2. Next, drop your shoulder and bend your knees.

3. Quickly, stand up and drive your fist upward and into the target. Your palm should be facing you when contact is made with the target. To avoid any possible injury, always keep your wrists straight.

4. Make certain your punch has a tight arc. Avoid "winding up" the blow. A properly executed uppercut punch should be a tight explosive jolt.

5. Return to the fighting stance.

The lead uppercut punch.

The rear uppercut.

Blocking Techniques

Blocks are defensive techniques designed to intercept your assailant's circular attacks. They are performed by placing a non-vital body part between the opponent's strike and your anatomical body target. There are three primary blocks you need to learn. They are:

- **high block**
- **mid block**
- **elbow block**

High Block

The high block is used to defend against overhead blows. To execute the lead high block, simply raise your lead arm up and extend your forearm out and above your head. Make certain that your hand is open and not clenched. This will increase the surface area of your block and provide a quick counterattack. The mechanics for the lead high block are the same as for the rear high block. Raise your rear arm up and extend your forearm out and above your head.

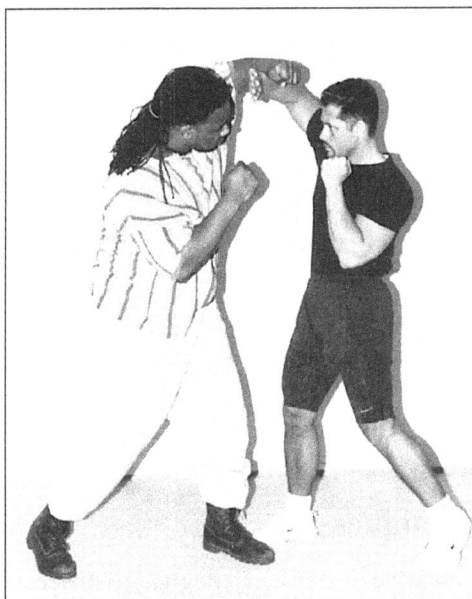

The high block.

Mid Block

The mid-block is specifically used to defend against circular blows to your head or upper torso. To perform the move, raise either your right or left arm at approximately 90 degrees while simultaneously pronating (rotating) it into the direction of the strike. Make contact with the belly of your forearm at the assailant's wrist or forearm. This movement will provide maximum structural integrity for the blocking tool. Make certain that your hand is held open to increase the surface area of your block. When performing the mid-block, be certain to time the rotation of your arm with the attack. Don't forget that the mid-block has both height (up and down) and width (in and out) fluctuations that are relative to the characteristics of the assailant's blow.

The lead hand mid block.

In this photo, a rear hand mid block.

The 10 Best Mental Toughness Exercises

Elbow Block

The elbow block is used to stop circular blows to your midsection, such as uppercuts, shovel hooks, and hook kicks. To execute the move, drop your elbow and simultaneously twist your body toward your centerline. Be certain to keep your elbow perpendicular to the floor with your hands relaxed and close to your chest. The elbow block can be used on both the right and left sides.

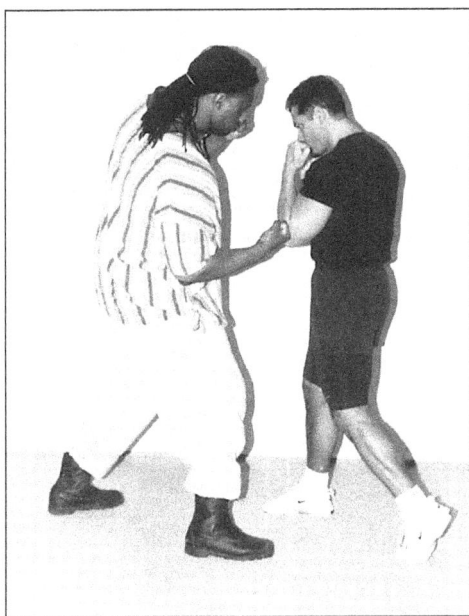

Pictured here, the elbow block.

Parrying Techniques

The parry is a quick, forceful slap that redirects your assailant's linear strike (jabs, lead straights, and rear crosses). There are two general types of parries, horizontal and vertical, and both can be performed with the right and left hands.

Horizontal Parry

To properly execute a horizontal parry from a fighting stance, move your lead hand horizontally across your body to deflect and redirect the assailant's punch. Immediately return to your guard position. Be certain to make contact with the palm of your hand.

Pictured here, a right hand horizontal parry.

Vertical Parry

To execute a vertical parry, from a fighting stance, move your hand vertically down your body to deflect and redirect the assailant's blow. Once again, don't forget to counterattack your opponent. A word of caution, don't parry punches with your finger. The fingers provide no structural integrity, and they can be jammed or broken easily.

The 10 Best Mental Toughness Exercises

Glossary

The following terms are defined in the context of Contemporary Fighting Arts and its related concepts. In many instances, the definitions bear little resemblance to those found in a standard dictionary.

A

accuracy—The precise or exact projection of force. Accuracy is also defined as the ability to execute a combative movement with precision and exactness.

adaptability—The ability to physically and psychologically adjust to new or different conditions or circumstances of combat.

advanced first-strike tools—Offensive techniques that are specifically used when confronted with multiple opponents.

aerobic exercise—Literally, "with air." Exercise that elevates the heart rate to a training level for a prolonged period of time, usually 30 minutes.

affective preparedness – One of the three components of preparedness. Affective preparedness means being emotionally, philosophically, and spiritually prepared for the strains of combat. See cognitive preparedness and psychomotor preparedness.

aggression—Hostile and injurious behavior directed toward a person.

aggressive response—One of the three possible counters when assaulted by a grab, choke, or hold from a standing position. Aggressive response requires you to counter the enemy with destructive blows and strikes. See moderate response and passive response.

aggressive hand positioning—Placement of hands so as to imply aggressive or hostile intentions.

agility—An attribute of combat. One's ability to move his or her body quickly and gracefully.

amalgamation—A scientific process of uniting or merging.

ambidextrous—The ability to perform with equal facility on both the right and left sides of the body.

anabolic steroids – synthetic chemical compounds that resemble the male sex hormone testosterone. This performance-enhancing drug is known to increase lean muscle mass, strength, and endurance.

analysis and integration—One of the five elements of CFA's mental component. This is the painstaking process of breaking down various elements, concepts, sciences, and disciplines into their atomic parts, and then methodically and strategically analyzing, experimenting, and drastically modifying the information so that it fulfills three combative requirements: efficiency, effectiveness, and safety. Only then is it finally integrated into the CFA system.

anatomical striking targets—The various anatomical body targets that can be struck and which are especially vulnerable to potential harm. They include: the eyes, temple, nose, chin, back of neck, front of neck, solar plexus, ribs, groin, thighs, knees, shins, and instep.

anchoring – The strategic process of trapping the assailant's neck or limb in order to control the range of engagement during razing.

assailant—A person who threatens or attacks another person.

assault—The threat or willful attempt to inflict injury upon the person of another.

assault and battery—The unlawful touching of another person without justification.

assessment—The process of rapidly gathering, analyzing, and accurately evaluating information in terms of threat and danger. You can assess people, places, actions, and objects.

attack—Offensive action designed to physically control, injure, or kill another person.

attack by combination (ABC) - One of the five methods of attack. See compound attack.

attack by drawing (ABD) - One of the five methods of attack. A method of attack predicated on counterattack.

attitude—One of the three factors that determine who wins a street fight. Attitude means being emotionally, philosophically, and spiritually liberated from societal and religious mores. See skills and knowledge.

attributes of combat—The physical, mental, and spiritual qualities that enhance combat skills and tactics.

awareness—Perception or knowledge of people, places, actions, and objects. (In CFA, there are three categories of tactical awareness: criminal awareness, situational awareness, and self-awareness.)

B

balance—One's ability to maintain equilibrium while stationary or moving.

blading the body—Strategically positioning your body at a 45-degree angle.

blitz and disengage—A style of sparring whereby a fighter moves into a range of combat, unleashes a strategic compound attack, and then quickly disengages to a safe distance. Of all sparring methodologies, the blitz and disengage most closely resembles a real street fight.

block—A defensive tool designed to intercept the assailant's attack by placing a non-vital target between the assailant's strike and your vital body target.

body composition—The ratio of fat to lean body tissue.

body language—Nonverbal communication through posture, gestures, and facial expressions.

body mechanics—Technically precise body movement during the execution of a body weapon, defensive technique, or other fighting maneuver.

body tackle – A tackle that occurs when your opponent haphazardly rushes forward and plows his body into yours.

body weapon—Also known as a tool, one of the various body parts that can be used to strike or otherwise injure or kill a criminal assailant.

burn out—A negative emotional state acquired by physically over- training. Some symptoms include: illness, boredom, anxiety, disinterest in training, and general sluggishness.

C

cadence—Coordinating tempo and rhythm to establish a timing pattern of movement.

cardiorespiratory conditioning—The component of physical fitness that deals with the heart, lungs, and circulatory system.

centerline—An imaginary vertical line that divides your body in half and which contains many of your vital anatomical targets.

choke holds—Holds that impair the flow of blood or oxygen to the brain.

circular movements—Movements that follow the direction of a curve.

close-quarter combat—One of the three ranges of knife and

bludgeon combat. At this distance, you can strike, slash, or stab your assailant with a variety of close-quarter techniques.

cognitive development—One of the five elements of CFA's mental component. The process of developing and enhancing your fighting skills through specific mental exercises and techniques. See analysis and integration, killer instinct, philosophy, and strategic/tactical development.

cognitive exercises—Various mental exercises used to enhance fighting skills and tactics.

cognitive preparedness – One of the three components of preparedness. Cognitive preparedness means being equipped with the strategic concepts, principles, and general knowledge of combat. See affective preparedness and psychomotor preparedness.

combat-oriented training—Training that is specifically related to the harsh realities of both armed and unarmed combat. See ritual-oriented training and sport-oriented training.

combative arts—The various arts of war. See martial arts.

combative attributes—See attributes of combat.

combative fitness—A state characterized by cardiorespiratory and muscular/skeletal conditioning, as well as proper body composition.

combative mentality—Also known as the killer instinct, this is a combative state of mind necessary for fighting. See killer instinct.

combat ranges—The various ranges of unarmed combat.

combative utility—The quality of condition of being combatively useful.

combination(s)—See compound attack.

common peroneal nerve—A pressure point area located approximately four to six inches above the knee on the midline of the outside of the thigh.

composure—A combative attribute. Composure is a quiet and focused mind-set that enables you to acquire your combative agenda.

compound attack—One of the five conventional methods of attack. Two or more body weapons launched in strategic succession whereby the fighter overwhelms his assailant with a flurry of full speed, full-force blows.

conditioning training—A CFA training methodology requiring the practitioner to deliver a variety of offensive and defensive combinations for a 4-minute period. See proficiency training and street training.

contact evasion—Physically moving or manipulating your body to avoid being tackled by the adversary.

Contemporary Fighting Arts—A modern martial art and self-defense system made up of three parts: physical, mental, and spiritual.

conventional ground-fighting tools—Specific ground-fighting techniques designed to control, restrain, and temporarily incapacitate your adversary. Some conventional ground fighting tactics include: submission holds, locks, certain choking techniques, and specific striking techniques.

coordination—A physical attribute characterized by the ability to perform a technique or movement with efficiency, balance, and accuracy.

counterattack—Offensive action made to counter an assailant's initial attack.

courage—A combative attribute. The state of mind and spirit that enables a fighter to face danger and vicissitudes with confidence, resolution, and bravery.

creatine monohydrate—A tasteless and odorless white powder that mimics some of the effects of anabolic steroids. Creatine is a safe body-building product that can benefit anyone who wants to increase their strength, endurance, and lean muscle mass.

criminal awareness—One of the three categories of CFA awareness. It involves a general understanding and knowledge of the nature and dynamics of a criminal's motivations, mentalities, methods, and capabilities to perpetrate violent crime. See situational awareness and self-awareness.

criminal justice—The study of criminal law and the procedures associated with its enforcement.

criminology—The scientific study of crime and criminals.

cross-stepping—The process of crossing one foot in front of or behind the other when moving.

crushing tactics—Nuclear grappling-range techniques designed to crush the assailant's anatomical targets.

D

deadly force—Weapons or techniques that may result in unconsciousness, permanent disfigurement, or death.

deception—A combative attribute. A stratagem whereby you delude your assailant.

decisiveness—A combative attribute. The ability to follow a tactical course of action that is unwavering and focused.

defense—The ability to strategically thwart an assailant's attack (armed or unarmed).

defensive flow—A progression of continuous defensive responses.

defensive mentality—A defensive mind-set.

defensive reaction time—The elapsed time between an assailant's physical attack and your defensive response to that attack. See offensive reaction time.

demeanor—A person's outward behavior. One of the essential factors to consider when assessing a threatening individual.

diet—A lifestyle of healthy eating.

disingenuous vocalization—The strategic and deceptive utilization of words to successfully launch a preemptive strike at your adversary.

distancing—The ability to quickly understand spatial relationships and how they relate to combat.

distractionary tactics—Various verbal and physical tactics designed to distract your adversary.

double-end bag—A small leather ball hung from the ceiling and anchored to the floor with bungee cord. It helps develop striking accuracy, speed, timing, eye-hand coordination, footwork and overall defensive skills.

double-leg takedown—A takedown that occurs when your opponent shoots for both of your legs to force you to the ground.

E

ectomorph—One of the three somatotypes. A body type characterized by a high degree of slenderness, angularity, and fragility. See endomorph and mesomorph.

effectiveness—One of the three criteria for a CFA body weapon, technique, tactic, or maneuver. It means the ability to produce a desired effect. See efficiency and safety.

efficiency—One of the three criteria for a CFA body weapon, technique, tactic, or maneuver. It means the ability to reach an objective quickly and economically. See effectiveness and safety.

emotionless—A combative attribute. Being temporarily devoid of human feeling.

endomorph—One of the three somatotypes. A body type characterized by a high degree of roundness, softness, and body fat. See ectomorph and mesomorph.

evasion—A defensive maneuver that allows you to strategically maneuver your body away from the assailant's strike.

evasive sidestepping—Evasive footwork where the practitioner moves to either the right or left side.

evasiveness—A combative attribute. The ability to avoid threat or danger.

excessive force—An amount of force that exceeds the need for a particular event and is unjustified in the eyes of the law.

experimentation—The painstaking process of testing a combative hypothesis or theory.

explosiveness—A combative attribute that is characterized by a sudden outburst of violent energy.

F

fear—A strong and unpleasant emotion caused by the anticipation or awareness of threat or danger. There are three stages of fear in order of intensity: fright, panic, and terror. See fright, panic, and terror.

feeder—A skilled technician who manipulates the focus mitts.

femoral nerve—A pressure point area located approximately 6 inches above the knee on the inside of the thigh.

fighting stance—Any one of the stances used in CFA's system. A strategic posture you can assume when face-to-face with an unarmed assailant(s). The fighting stance is generally used after you have launched your first-strike tool.

fight-or-flight syndrome—A response of the sympathetic nervous system to a fearful and threatening situation, during which it prepares your body to either fight or flee from the perceived danger.

finesse—A combative attribute. The ability to skillfully execute a movement or a series of movements with grace and refinement.

first strike—Proactive force used to interrupt the initial stages of an assault before it becomes a self-defense situation.

first-strike principle—A CFA principle that states that when physical danger is imminent and you have no other tactical option but to fight back, you should strike first, strike fast, and strike with authority and keep the pressure on.

first-strike stance—One of the stances used in CFA's system. A strategic posture used prior to initiating a first strike.

first-strike tools—Specific offensive tools designed to initiate a preemptive strike against your adversary.

fisted blows – Hand blows delivered with a clenched fist.

five tactical options – The five strategic responses you can make in a self-defense situation, listed in order of increasing level of resistance: comply, escape, de-escalate, assert, and fight back.

flexibility—The muscles' ability to move through maximum natural ranges. See muscular/skeletal conditioning.

focus mitts—Durable leather hand mitts used to develop and sharpen offensive and defensive skills.

footwork—Quick, economical steps performed on the balls of the feet while you are relaxed, alert, and balanced. Footwork is structured around four general movements: forward, backward, right, and left.

fractal tool—Offensive or defensive tools that can be used in more than one combat range.

fright—The first stage of fear; quick and sudden fear. See panic and terror.

full Beat – One of the four beat classifications in the Widow Maker Program. The full beat strike has a complete initiation and retraction phase.

G

going postal - a slang term referring to a person who suddenly and unexpectedly attacks you with an explosive and frenzied flurry of blows. Also known as postal attack.

grappling range—One of the three ranges of unarmed combat. Grappling range is the closest distance of unarmed combat from which you can employ a wide variety of close-quarter tools and techniques. The grappling range of unarmed combat is also divided into two planes: vertical (standing) and horizontal (ground fighting). See kicking range and punching range.

grappling-range tools—The various body tools and techniques that are employed in the grappling range of unarmed combat, including head butts; biting, tearing, clawing, crushing, and gouging tactics; foot stomps, horizontal, vertical, and diagonal elbow strikes, vertical and diagonal knee strikes, chokes, strangles, joint locks, and holds. See punching range tools and kicking range tools.

ground fighting—Also known as the horizontal grappling plane, this is fighting that takes place on the ground.

guard—Also known as the hand guard, this refers to a fighter's hand positioning.

guard position—Also known as leg guard or scissors hold, this is a ground-fighting position in which a fighter is on his back holding his opponent between his legs.

H

half beat – One of the four beat classifications in the Widow Maker Program. The half beat strike is delivered through the retraction phase of the proceeding strike.

hand immobilization attack (HIA) - One of the five methods of attack. A method of attack whereby the practitioner traps his opponent's limb or limbs in order to execute an offense attack of his own.

hand positioning—See guard.

hand wraps—Long strips of cotton that are wrapped around the hands and wrists for greater protection.

haymaker—A wild and telegraphed swing of the arms executed by an unskilled fighter.

head-hunter—A fighter who primarily attacks the head.

heavy bag—A large cylindrical bag used to develop kicking, punching, or striking power.

high-line kick—One of the two different classifications of a kick. A kick that is directed to targets above an assailant's waist level. See low-line kick.

hip fusing—A full-contact drill that teaches a fighter to "stand his ground" and overcome the fear of exchanging blows with a stronger opponent. This exercise is performed by connecting two fighters with a 3-foot chain, forcing them to fight in the punching range of unarmed combat.

histrionics—The field of theatrics or acting.

hook kick—A circular kick that can be delivered in both kicking and punching ranges.

hook punch—A circular punch that can be delivered in both the punching and grappling ranges.

I

impact power—Destructive force generated by mass and velocity.

impact training—A training exercise that develops pain tolerance.

incapacitate—To disable an assailant by rendering him unconscious or damaging his bones, joints, or organs.

initiative—Making the first offensive move in combat.

inside position—The area between the opponent's arms, where he has the greatest amount of control.

intent—One of the essential factors to consider when assessing a threatening individual. The assailant's purpose or motive. See demeanor, positioning, range, and weapon capability.

intuition—The innate ability to know or sense something without the use of rational thought.

J

jeet kune do (JKD) - "Way of the intercepting fist." Bruce Lee's approach to the martial arts, which includes his innovative concepts, theories, methodologies, and philosophies.

jersey Pull – Strategically pulling the assailant's shirt or jacket over his head as he disengages from the clinch position.

joint lock—A grappling-range technique that immobilizes the assailant's joint.

K

kick—A sudden, forceful strike with the foot.

kicking range—One of the three ranges of unarmed combat. Kicking range is the furthest distance of unarmed combat wherein you use your legs to strike an assailant. See grappling range and punching range.

kicking-range tools—The various body weapons employed in the kicking range of unarmed combat, including side kicks, push kicks, hook kicks, and vertical kicks.

killer instinct—A cold, primal mentality that surges to your consciousness and turns you into a vicious fighter.

kinesics—The study of nonlinguistic body movement communications. (For example, eye movement, shrugs, or facial gestures.)

kinesiology—The study of principles and mechanics of human movement.

kinesthetic perception—The ability to accurately feel your body during the execution of a particular movement.

knowledge—One of the three factors that determine who will win a street fight. Knowledge means knowing and understanding how to fight. See skills and attitude.

L

lead side -The side of the body that faces an assailant.

leg guard—See guard position.

linear movement—Movements that follow the path of a straight line.

low-maintenance tool—Offensive and defensive tools that require the least amount of training and practice to maintain proficiency. Low maintenance tools generally do not require preliminary stretching.

low-line kick—One of the two different classifications of a kick. A kick that is directed to targets below the assailant's waist level. (See high-line kick.)

lock—See joint lock.

M

maneuver—To manipulate into a strategically desired position.

MAP—An acronym that stands for moderate, aggressive, passive. MAP provides the practitioner with three possible responses to various grabs, chokes, and holds that occur from a standing position. See aggressive response, moderate response, and passive response.

martial arts—The "arts of war."

masking—The process of concealing your true feelings from your opponent by manipulating and managing your body language.

mechanics—(See body mechanics.)

mental attributes—The various cognitive qualities that enhance your fighting skills.

mental component—One of the three vital components of the CFA system. The mental component includes the cerebral aspects of fighting including the killer instinct, strategic and tactical development, analysis and integration, philosophy, and cognitive development. See physical component and spiritual component.

mesomorph—One of the three somatotypes. A body type classified by a high degree of muscularity and strength. The mesomorph possesses the ideal physique for unarmed combat. See ectomorph and endomorph.

mobility—A combative attribute. The ability to move your body quickly and freely while balanced. See footwork.

moderate response—One of the three possible counters when assaulted by a grab, choke, or hold from a standing position. Moderate response requires you to counter your opponent with a control and restraint (submission hold). See aggressive response and passive response.

modern martial art—A pragmatic combat art that has evolved to meet the demands and characteristics of the present time.

mounted position—A dominant ground-fighting position where a fighter straddles his opponent.

muscular endurance—The muscles' ability to perform the same motion or task repeatedly for a prolonged period of time.

muscular flexibility—The muscles' ability to move through maximum natural ranges.

muscular strength—The maximum force that can be exerted by a particular muscle or muscle group against resistance.

muscular/skeletal conditioning—An element of physical fitness that entails muscular strength, endurance, and flexibility.

N

naked choke—A throat choke executed from the chest to back position. This secure choke is executed with two hands and it can be performed while standing, kneeling, and ground fighting with the opponent.

neck crush – A powerful pain compliance technique used when the adversary buries his head in your chest to avoid being razed.

neutralize—See incapacitate.

neutral zone—The distance outside the kicking range at which neither the practitioner nor the assailant can touch the other.

nonaggressive physiology—Strategic body language used prior to initiating a first strike.

nontelegraphic movement—Body mechanics or movements that do not inform an assailant of your intentions.

nuclear ground-fighting tools—Specific grappling range tools designed to inflict immediate and irreversible damage. Nuclear tools and tactics include biting tactics, tearing tactics, crushing tactics, continuous choking tactics, gouging techniques, raking tactics, and all striking techniques.

O

offense—The armed and unarmed means and methods of attacking a criminal assailant.

offensive flow—Continuous offensive movements (kicks, blows, and strikes) with unbroken continuity that ultimately neutralize or terminate the opponent. See compound attack.

offensive reaction time—The elapsed time between target selection and target impaction.

one-mindedness—A state of deep concentration wherein you are free from all distractions (internal and external).

ostrich defense—One of the biggest mistakes one can make when defending against an opponent. This is when the practitioner looks away from that which he fears (punches, kicks, and strikes). His mentality is, "If I can't see it, it can't hurt me."

P

pain tolerance—Your ability to physically and psychologically withstand pain.

panic—The second stage of fear; overpowering fear. See fright and terror.

parry—A defensive technique: a quick, forceful slap that redirects an assailant's linear attack. There are two types of parries: horizontal and vertical.

passive response—One of the three possible counters when assaulted by a grab, choke, or hold from a standing position. Passive response requires you to nullify the assault without injuring your adversary. See aggressive response and moderate response.

patience—A combative attribute. The ability to endure and tolerate difficulty.

perception—Interpretation of vital information acquired from your senses when faced with a potentially threatening situation.

philosophical resolution—The act of analyzing and answering various questions concerning the use of violence in defense of yourself and others.

philosophy—One of the five aspects of CFA's mental component. A deep state of introspection whereby you methodically resolve critical questions concerning the use of force in defense of yourself or others.

physical attributes—The numerous physical qualities that enhance your combative skills and abilities.

physical component—One of the three vital components of the CFA system. The physical component includes the physical aspects of fighting, such as physical fitness, weapon/technique mastery, and combative attributes. See mental component and spiritual component.

physical conditioning—See combative fitness.

physical fitness—See combative fitness.

positional asphyxia—The arrangement, placement, or positioning of your opponent's body in such a way as to interrupt your breathing and cause unconsciousness or possibly death.

positioning—The spatial relationship of the assailant to the assailed person in terms of target exposure, escape, angle of attack, and various other strategic considerations.

postal attack - see going postal.

power—A physical attribute of armed and unarmed combat. The amount of force you can generate when striking an anatomical target.

power generators—Specific points on your body that generate impact power. There are three anatomical power generators: shoulders, hips, and feet.

precision—See accuracy.

preemptive strike—See first strike.

premise—An axiom, concept, rule, or any other valid reason to modify or go beyond that which has been established.

preparedness—A state of being ready for combat. There are three components of preparedness: affective preparedness, cognitive preparedness, and psychomotor preparedness.

probable reaction dynamics - The opponent's anticipated or predicted movements or actions during both armed and unarmed combat.

proficiency training—A CFA training methodology requiring the practitioner to execute a specific body weapon, technique, maneuver, or tactic over and over for a prescribed number of repetitions. See conditioning training and street training.

progressive indirect attack (PIA) – One of the five methods of attack. A progressive method of attack whereby the initial tool or technique is designed to set the opponent up for follow-up blows.

proxemics—The study of the nature and effect of man's personal space.

proximity—The ability to maintain a strategically safe distance from a threatening individual.

pseudospeciation—A combative attribute. The tendency to assign subhuman and inferior qualities to a threatening assailant.

psychological conditioning—The process of conditioning the mind for the horrors and rigors of real combat.

psychomotor preparedness—One of the three components of preparedness. Psychomotor preparedness means possessing all of the physical skills and attributes necessary to defeat a formidable adversary. See affective preparedness and cognitive preparedness.

punch—A quick, forceful strike of the fists.

punching range—One of the three ranges of unarmed combat. Punching range is the mid range of unarmed combat from which the fighter uses his hands to strike his assailant. See kicking range and grappling range.

punching-range tools—The various body weapons that are employed in the punching range of unarmed combat, including finger jabs, palm-heel strikes, rear cross, knife-hand strikes, horizontal and shovel hooks, uppercuts, and hammer-fist strikes. See grappling-range tools and kicking-range tools.

Q

qualities of combat—See attributes of combat.

quarter beat - One of the four beat classifications of the Widow Maker Program. Quarter beat strikes never break contact with the assailant's face. Quarter beat strikes are primarily responsible for creating the psychological panic and trauma when Razing.

R

range—The spatial relationship between a fighter and a threatening assailant.

range deficiency—The inability to effectively fight and defend in all ranges of combat (armed and unarmed).

range manipulation—A combative attribute. The strategic manipulation of combat ranges.

range proficiency—A combative attribute. The ability to effectively fight and defend in all ranges of combat (armed and unarmed).

ranges of engagement—See combat ranges.

ranges of unarmed combat—The three distances (kicking range, punching range, and grappling range) a fighter might physically engage with an assailant while involved in unarmed combat.

raze – To level, demolish or obliterate.

razer – One who performs the Razing methodology.

razing – The second phase of the Widow Maker Program. A series of vicious close quarter techniques designed to physically and psychologically extirpate a criminal attacker.

razing amplifier - a technique, tactic or procedure that magnifies the destructiveness of your razing technique.

reaction dynamics—see probable reaction dynamics.

reaction time—The elapsed time between a stimulus and the response to that particular stimulus. See offensive reaction time and defensive reaction time.

rear cross—A straight punch delivered from the rear hand that crosses from right to left (if in a left stance) or left to right (if in a right stance).

rear side—The side of the body furthest from the assailant. See lead side.

reasonable force—That degree of force which is not excessive for a particular event and which is appropriate in protecting yourself or others.

refinement—The strategic and methodical process of improving or perfecting.

relocation principle—Also known as relocating, this is a street-fighting tactic that requires you to immediately move to a new location (usually by flanking your adversary) after delivering a compound attack.

repetition—Performing a single movement, exercise, strike, or action continuously for a specific period.

research—A scientific investigation or inquiry.

rhythm—Movements characterized by the natural ebb and flow of related elements.

ritual-oriented training—Formalized training that is conducted without intrinsic purpose. See combat-oriented training and sport-oriented training.

S

safety—One of the three criteria for a CFA body weapon, technique, maneuver, or tactic. It means that the tool, technique, maneuver or tactic provides the least amount of danger and risk for the practitioner. See efficiency and effectiveness.

scissors hold—See guard position.

scorching – Quickly and inconspicuously applying oleoresin capsicum (hot pepper extract) on your fingertips and then razing your adversary.

self-awareness—One of the three categories of CFA awareness. Knowing and understanding yourself. This includes aspects of yourself which may provoke criminal violence and which will promote a proper and strong reaction to an attack. See criminal awareness and situational awareness.

self-confidence—Having trust and faith in yourself.

self-enlightenment—The state of knowing your capabilities, limitations, character traits, feelings, general attributes, and motivations. See self-awareness.

set—A term used to describe a grouping of repetitions.

shadow fighting—A CFA training exercise used to develop and refine your tools, techniques, and attributes of armed and unarmed combat.

sharking – A counter attack technique that is used when your adversary grabs your razing hand.

shielding wedge - a defensive maneuver used to counter an unarmed postal attack.

simple direct attack (SDA) – One of the five methods of attack. A method of attack whereby the practitioner delivers a solitary offenses tool or technique. It may involve a series of discrete probes or one swift, powerful strike aimed at terminating the encounter.

situational awareness—One of the three categories of CFA awareness. A state of being totally alert to your immediate surroundings, including people, places, objects, and actions. (See criminal awareness and self-awareness.)

skeletal alignment—The proper alignment or arrangement of your body. Skeletal alignment maximizes the structural integrity of striking tools.

skills—One of the three factors that determine who will win a street fight. Skills refers to psychomotor proficiency with the tools and techniques of combat. See Attitude and Knowledge.

slipping—A defensive maneuver that permits you to avoid an assailant's linear blow without stepping out of range. Slipping can be accomplished by quickly snapping the head and upper torso sideways (right or left) to avoid the blow.

snap back—A defensive maneuver that permits you to avoid an assailant's linear and circular blows without stepping out of range. The snap back can be accomplished by quickly snapping the head backward to avoid the assailant's blow.

somatotypes—A method of classifying human body types or builds into three different categories: endomorph, mesomorph, and ectomorph. See endomorph, mesomorph, and ectomorph.

sparring—A training exercise where two or more fighters fight each other while wearing protective equipment.

speed—A physical attribute of armed and unarmed combat. The rate or a measure of the rapid rate of motion.

spiritual component—One of the three vital components of the CFA system. The spiritual component includes the metaphysical issues and aspects of existence. See physical component and mental component.

sport-oriented training—Training that is geared for competition and governed by a set of rules. See combat-oriented training and ritual-oriented training.

sprawling—A grappling technique used to counter a double- or single-leg takedown.

square off—To be face-to-face with a hostile or threatening assailant who is about to attack you.

stance—One of the many strategic postures you assume prior to or during armed or unarmed combat.

stick fighting—Fighting that takes place with either one or two sticks.

strategic positioning—Tactically positioning yourself to either escape, move behind a barrier, or use a makeshift weapon.

strategic/tactical development—One of the five elements of CFA's mental component.

strategy—A carefully planned method of achieving your goal of engaging an assailant under advantageous conditions.

street fight—A spontaneous and violent confrontation between two or more individuals wherein no rules apply.

street fighter—An unorthodox combatant who has no formal training. His combative skills and tactics are usually developed in the street by the process of trial and error.

street training—A CFA training methodology requiring the practitioner to deliver explosive compound attacks for 10 to 20 seconds. See condition ng training and proficiency training.

strength training—The process of developing muscular strength through systematic application of progressive resistance.

striking art—A combat art that relies predominantly on striking techniques to neutralize or terminate a criminal attacker.

striking shield—A rectangular shield constructed of foam and vinyl used to develop power in your kicks, punches, and strikes.

striking tool—A natural body weapon that impacts with the assailant's anatomical target.

strong side—The strongest and most coordinated side of your body.

structure—A definite and organized pattern.

style—The distinct manner in which a fighter executes or performs his combat skills.

stylistic integration—The purposeful and scientific collection of tools and techniques from various disciplines, which are strategically integrated and dramatically altered to meet three essential criteria: efficiency, effectiveness, and combative safety.

submission holds—Also known as control and restraint techniques, many of these locks and holds create sufficient pain to cause the adversary to submit.

system—The unification of principles, philosophies, rules, strategies, methodologies, tools, and techniques of a particular method of combat.

T

tactic—The skill of using the available means to achieve an end.

target awareness—A combative attribute that encompasses five strategic principles: target orientation, target recognition, target selection, target impaction, and target exploitation.

target exploitation—A combative attribute. The strategic maximization of your assailant's reaction dynamics during a fight. Target exploitation can be applied in both armed and unarmed encounters.

target impaction—The successful striking of the appropriate anatomical target.

target orientation—A combative attribute. Having a workable knowledge of the assailant's anatomical targets.

target recognition—The ability to immediately recognize appropriate anatomical targets during an emergency self-defense situation.

target selection—The process of mentally selecting the appropriate anatomical target for your self-defense situation. This is predicated on certain factors, including proper force response, assailant's positioning, and range.

target stare—A form of telegraphing in which you stare at the anatomical target you intend to strike.

target zones—The three areas in which an assailant's anatomical targets are located. (See zone one, zone two and zone three.)

technique—A systematic procedure by which a task is accomplished.

telegraphic cognizance—A combative attribute. The ability to recognize both verbal and non-verbal signs of aggression or assault.

telegraphing—Unintentionally making your intentions known to your adversary.

tempo—The speed or rate at which you speak.

terminate—To kill.

terror—The third stage of fear; defined as overpowering fear. See fright and panic.

timing—A physical and mental attribute of armed and unarmed combat. Your ability to execute a movement at the optimum moment.

tone—The overall quality or character of your voice.

tool—See body weapon.

traditional martial arts—Any martial art that fails to evolve and change to meet the demands and characteristics of its present environment.

traditional style/system—See traditional martial arts.

training drills—The various exercises and drills aimed at perfecting combat skills, attributes, and tactics.

trap and tuck – A counter move technique used when the adversary attempts to raze you during your quarter beat assault.

U

unified mind—A mind free and clear of distractions and focused on the combative situation.

use of force response—A combative attribute. Selecting the appropriate level of force for a particular emergency self-defense situation.

V

viciousness—A combative attribute. The propensity to be extremely violent and destructive often characterized by intense savagery.

violence—The intentional utilization of physical force to coerce, injure, cripple, or kill.

visualization—Also known as mental visualization or mental imagery. The purposeful formation of mental images and scenarios in the mind's eye.

W

warm-up—A series of mild exercises, stretches, and movements designed to prepare you for more intense exercise.

weak side—The weaker and more uncoordinated side of your body.

weapon and technique mastery—A component of CFA's physical component. The kinesthetic and psychomotor development of a weapon or combative technique.

weapon capability—An assailant's ability to use and attack with a particular weapon.

webbing - The first phase of the Widow Maker Program. Webbing is a two hand strike delivered to the assailant's chin. It is called Webbing because your hands resemble a large web that wraps around the enemy's face.

widow maker – One who makes widows by destroying husbands.

widow maker program – A CFA combat program specifically designed to teach the law abiding citizen how to use extreme force when faced with immediate threat of unlawful deadly criminal attack. The Widow Maker program is divided into two phases or methodologies: Webbing and Razing.

Y

yell—A loud and aggressive scream or shout used for various strategic reasons.

Z

zero beat – One of the four beat classifications of the Widow Maker, Feral Fighting and Savage Street Fighting Programs. Zero beat strikes are full pressure techniques applied to a specific target until it completely ruptures. They include gouging, crushing, biting, and choking techniques.

zone one—Anatomical targets related to your senses, including the eyes, temple, nose, chin, and back of neck.

zone three—Anatomical targets related to your mobility, including thighs, knees, shins, and instep.

zone two—Anatomical targets related to your breathing, including front of neck, solar plexus, ribs, and groin.

About Sammy Franco

With over 30 years of experience, Sammy Franco is one of the world's foremost authorities on armed and unarmed self-defense. Highly regarded as a leading innovator in combat sciences, Mr. Franco was one of the premier pioneers in the field of "reality-based" self-defense and martial arts instruction.

Sammy Franco is perhaps best known as the founder and creator of Contemporary Fighting Arts (CFA), a state-of-the-art offensive-based combat system that is specifically designed for real-world self-defense. CFA is a sophisticated and practical system of self-defense, designed specifically to provide efficient and effective methods to avoid, defuse, confront, and neutralize both armed and unarmed attackers.

Sammy Franco has frequently been featured in martial art magazines, newspapers, and appeared on numerous radio and television programs. Mr. Franco has also authored numerous books, magazine articles, and editorials, and has developed a popular library of instructional videos.

Sammy Franco's experience and credibility in the combat sciences is unequaled. One of his many accomplishments in this field includes the fact that he has earned the ranking of a Law Enforcement Master Instructor, and has designed, implemented, and taught officer survival training to the United States Border Patrol (USBP). He has instructed members of the US Secret Service, Military Special Forces,

The 10 Best Mental Toughness Exercises

Washington DC Police Department, Montgomery County, Maryland Deputy Sheriffs, and the US Library of Congress Police. Sammy Franco is also a member of the prestigious International Law Enforcement Educators and Trainers Association (ILEETA) as well as the American Society of Law Enforcement Trainers (ASLET) and he is listed in the "Who's Who Director of Law Enforcement Instructors."

Sammy Franco is a nationally certified Law Enforcement Instructor in the following curricula: PR-24 Side-Handle Baton, Police Arrest and Control Procedures, Police Personal Weapons Tactics, Police Power Handcuffing Methods, Police Oleoresin Capsicum Aerosol Training (OCAT), Police Weapon Retention and Disarming Methods, Police Edged Weapon Countermeasures and "Use of Force" Assessment and Response Methods.

Mr. Franco holds a Bachelor of Arts degree in Criminal Justice from the University of Maryland. He is a regularly featured speaker at a number of professional conferences and conducts dynamic and enlightening seminars on numerous aspects of self-defense and combat training.

On a personal level, Sammy Franco is an animal lover, who will go to great lengths to assist and rescue animals. Throughout the years, he's rescued everything from turkey vultures to goats. However, his most treasured moments are always spent with his beloved German Shepherd dogs.

For more information about Mr. Franco and his unique Contemporary Fighting Arts system, you can visit his website at: **SammyFranco.com** or follow him on twitter **@RealSammyFranco**

Other Books by Sammy Franco

KILLER INSTINCT
Unarmed Combat for Street Survival
by Sammy Franco

Here, Mr. Franco describes the mental, spiritual and physical components of his advanced system of combat that offers the fighter a brutal and efficient arsenal. But a weapon is only as good as the soldier trained to use it. Reading this book is the first step. Followed by proper and consistent training, the tools and techniques contained herein can be maximized by the martial artists who has attained self-knowledge, psychological preparedness and most importantly, mastery of the killer instinct. 8.5 x 5.5, paperback, photos, illus, 134 pages.

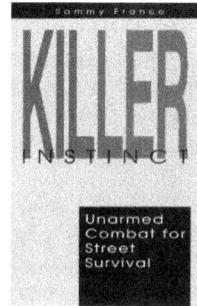

INVINCIBLE
Mental Toughness Techniques for Peak Performance
by Sammy Franco

Invincible is a treasure trove of battle-tested techniques and strategies for improving mental toughness in all aspects of life. It teaches you how to unlock the true power of your mind and achieve success in sports, fitness, high-risk professions, self-defense, and other peak performance activities. However, you don't have to be an athlete or warrior to benefit from this unique mental toughness book. In fact, the mental skills featured in this indispensable program can be used by anyone who wants to reach their full potential in life. 8.5 x 5.5, paperback, photos, illus, 250 pages.

WARRIOR WISDOM
Inspiring Ideas from the World's Greatest Warriors
by Sammy Franco

Warrior Wisdom includes a huge collection of unforgettable quotes, sayings and writings from warriors and warrior leaders, both past and present, and from around the world. This exhaustive book reveals the essentialities of the Fighter's life, speaking with great heart, eloquence, wisdom and an earned authenticity on subjects still crucial to you today: leadership, loyalty, honor, courage, tactics, strategy and much more. Warrior Wisdom offers a unique opportunity to thoroughly explore what it really means to be a warrior...in the worlds of yesterday and today! 7 x 10, paperback, 216 pages.

141

SAVAGE STREET FIGHTING
Tactical Savagery as a Last Resort
by Sammy Franco

In this revolutionary book, Sammy Franco reveals the science behind his most primal street fighting method. Savage Street Fighting is a brutal self-defense system specifically designed to teach the law-abiding citizen how to use "Tactical Savagery" when faced with the immediate threat of an unlawful deadly criminal attack. Savage Street Fighting is systematically engineered to protect you when there are no other self-defense options left! With over 300 photographs and detailed step-by-step instructions, Savage Street Fighting is a must-have book for anyone concerned about real world self-defense. Now is the time to learn how to unleash your inner beast! 8.5 x 5.5, paperback, 317 photos, illustrations, 232 pages.

FIRST STRIKE
End a Fight in Ten Seconds or Less!
by Sammy Franco

Learn how to stop any attack before it starts by mastering the art of the preemptive strike. First Strike gives you an easy-to-learn yet highly effective self-defense game plan for handling violent close-quarter combat encounters. First Strike will teach you instinctive, practical and realistic self-defense techniques that will drop any criminal attacker to the floor with one punishing blow. By reading this book and by practicing, you will learn the hard-hitting skills necessary to execute a punishing first strike and ultimately prevail in a self-defense situation. And that's what it is all about: winning in as little time as possible. 8.5 x 5.5, paperback, photos, illustrations, 202 pages.

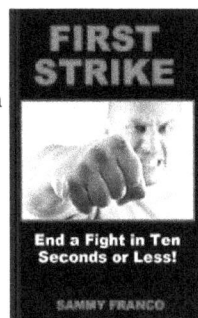

WAR MACHINE
How to Transform Yourself Into A Vicious & Deadly Street Fighter
by Sammy Franco

War Machine is a book that will change you for the rest of your life! When followed accordingly, War Machine will forge your mind, body and spirit into iron. Once armed with the mental and physical attributes of the War Machine, you will become a strong and confident warrior that can handle just about anything that life may throw your way. In essence, War Machine is a way of life. Powerful, intense, and hard. 11 x 8.5, paperback, photos, illustrations, 210 pages.

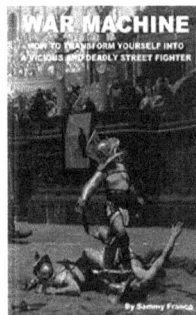

KUBOTAN POWER
Quick and Simple Steps to Mastering the Kubotan Keychain
by Sammy Franco

With over 290 photographs and step-by-step instructions, Kubotan Power is the authoritative resource for mastering this devastating self-defense weapon. In this one-of-a-kind book, world-renowned self-defense expert, Sammy Franco takes thirty years of real-world teaching experience and gives you quick, easy and practical kubotan techniques that can be used by civilians, law enforcement personnel, or military professionals. The Kubotan is an incredible self-defense weapon that has helped thousands of people effectively defend themselves. Men, women, law enforcement officers, military, and security professionals alike, appreciate this small and discreet self-defense tool. Unfortunately, however, very little has been written about the kubotan, leaving it shrouded in both mystery and ignorance. As a result, most people don't know how to unleash the full power of this unique personal defense weapon. 8.5 x 5.5, paperback, 290 photos, illustrations, 204 pages.

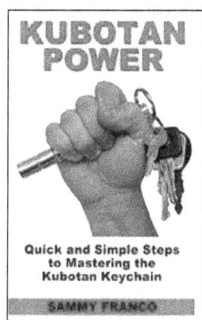

THE COMPLETE BODY OPPONENT BAG BOOK
by Sammy Franco

In this one-of-a-kind book, Sammy Franco teaches you the many hidden training features of the body opponent bag that will improve your fighting skills and boost your conditioning. With detailed photographs, step-by-step instructions, and dozens of unique workout routines, The Complete Body Opponent Bag Book is the authoritative resource for mastering this lifelike punching bag. The Complete Body Opponent Bag Book covers stances, punching, kicking, grappling techniques, mobility and footwork, targets, fighting ranges, training gear, time based workouts, punching and kicking combinations, weapons training, grappling drills, ground fighting, and dozens of workouts that will challenge you for years to come. 8.5 x 5.5, paperback, 139 photos, illustrations, 206 pages.

143